Introduc

"Oh, no! Not another Sunday afternoon at Au.

Visions of my childhood in Welwyn Garden City came rushing back, as I recalled the endless hours of my life being wasted, sitting quietly listening to the relentless ticking of a clock and the chattering of my Auntie.

"Why is he so big?" she would question, her voice piercing the silence.

"Well," replied my Dad.

"It's because he eats a lot of bread pudding."

"Is that true Dad?" I would ask when we finally found the refuge of home.

"Am I big because I eat lots of bread pudding?"

"No son, the bread pudding was just a quick answer for your Auntie Nellie. The real reason you are big is because I give you lots of loving."

Lots of loving ! What a marvellous answer.

Even today, as I sit down to write a few memories of my life, these words from childhood still ring in my ears. If we want to grow big, we need to know that we are loved! Human hearts everywhere are crying out for love. The soul shrinks for want of love. Every child needs the love of his Dad, and, in the same way, God - our heavenly Father, longs to pour out his eternal love into our hearts. It is not the 'pudding' of religion, good works or legalism which brings life, but rather the free gift of God's gracious love which energises us. It is this love which has been the dynamic foundation and continual heartbeat of my life. In the pages that follow, I would like to unfold something of the wonderful grace of God and encourage you to open up your own heart to more of His personal love for you.

I wrote this book many years ago when I was still in the innocent *"first love"* of my vocation. Come and join me in taking these *"steps of innocence."*

Steps of Innocence

A Journey of Grace and Love

Robert Reeve

DEDICATION

To my parents – both natural and spiritual, and to my children, David, Marc, Déborah and Myriam. In homage to my wider mission family as well, who are serving God's purpose in the world – the best wine is yet to come.

Contents

1 Caught by Love

A young Welsh boy wandered alone in the playground of the 'Barnardo's' Home in Cardiff. After the death of his Mum, he and the others in the family had struggled so hard to stay together, to survive, and to make sure the dinner was cooked and the house cleaned up. The boy remembered watching in wonder as his Dad used to take out a battered half-penny and spin it on the table. He would call it his *"lucky half-penny"* as, nestled fortuitously in his breast pocket, it had diverted a bullet from entering his young heart as he waged war in France. Destiny hangs on such slender threads ! When Dad became ill and died, all that effort to keep the family together seemed to have been wasted. The various elder brothers and sisters went their own ways, leaving the younger ones to fend for themselves in various orphanages.

At the age of just thirteen, the weight of the world seemed to be on his shoulders as he struggled to find some meaning to it all. They had been a poor family, but at least they had been a family. He remembered how he used to look down on the 'Barnardo Boys' because he felt he was at least better off than they were. But, oh the shame and the pain, to find that he was now himself a 'Barnardo's Boy'! He hated it. The five-pound note he received as his part of the inheritance seemed to add insult to injury. In the middle of one rebellious night, holding the lighted match to the sum total of what his family had bequeathed to him, he watched the flames consume the paper and felt his own heart burning to a dry ash.

"Oh God, I feel so alone!" he thought, turning his eyes heavenward.

Mysteriously, a strange desire to pray invaded his heart.

"Oh God, when I grow up, will you give me my own family? I'd love to be a Dad, and to be the father of boys. In fact I'd like to ask you for twin boys."

The wind blew through the playground as the bell rang to go in for lunch, but somehow things were different. A sense of eternity hung in the air and, almost despite himself, a heart had come to life again in the inspired environment of a prayer.

What a strange prayer though! Asking for twin boys is not usually the number one priority on most 13-year-old boys' prayer lists! And yet, the prayer was very real and became a kind of compass setting for the years to follow.

The folks were kind enough at the orphanage but the boy could never get over the sense of being a victim of charity which he resented strongly. The resentment boiled over into lots of fighting and shouting and even to an attempted arson of the school!

"We'd better batter the rebellion out of him," thought the authorities.

He found himself learning to box. Unfortunately, he was up against a rather large black man who, in a few lethal punches, knocked him out. The freezing cold water, which was thrown over him, may have brought him back to his senses, but it also gave him pleurisy, which nearly sent him to the grave.

The boy grew up in the school of hard knocks. As soon as he could, he left Barnardo's to work in a dairy and a shredded wheat factory. One night, walking the streets homeless, he was taken in by a family who gave him lodgings for the next few years.

Military Service came and went, as did an apprenticeship with the Eastern Electricity Board to become a cable jointer. And the romance! At a dance one evening, he saw a young lady and said to his friend.

"The lady I'm going to dance with will be my wife."

He danced with her. A whole year passed before they met again. They began to go out together. However, the man had another love in his life - not another woman, but a love, or rather a compulsion, for gambling. One night at the cinema, he told her that he had put all their money on a horse.

"It's bound to win," he said confidently.

Thankfully it didn't win, and the loss brought with it the revelation of the utter waste of gambling. The choice was made, no more gambling. His heart was set free to marry.

On the night of the honeymoon, he said to his new bride,

"We are going to have twins."

How would you react? Well, three months later the wife realised that she was indeed pregnant. The doctors said,

"No, it's not twins, there is only one heart beating."

But the young Welsh husband said,

"I'm sure it's twins!"

Later on, the doctors discovered that it was indeed twins and that the one heartbeat they heard was in fact two hearts beating together in unison. However, around the seven month period, there were some complications and the woman needed to give birth prematurely.

Two tiny, identical twin boys entered the world weighing no more than a bag of sugar each. Even at the very dawn of their lives, death seemed to be trying to smother away the breath of life. One of the boys had great difficulty breathing as his lungs were not fully working, whilst the other would not eat, seemingly being too weak to even have the will to live. Both boys were put into incubators with various breathing and feeding tubes.

On hearing the news of the birth, the father rushed to the hospital. Through the corridor window he saw the two little babies under the antiseptic glass of the incubators. Not knowing that they were his children, his heart went out to them.

He turned to a nurse and asked,

"Where are my boys?"

"Over there!" she replied, pointing to the incubators.

"I'm afraid there's not much chance of them surviving."

A priest was quickly called in so that they could be christened and fitted for heaven. However, another more fatherly heart was wanting them to be launched into life. This presented another challenge for our young Welshman who, at the very point of seeing his life's prayer come to fruition, was face to face with its utter destruction.

Quietly, with determination, he went over to the incubators, opened them up and took the two tiny little hands in his own.

"Live, live!" he willed in the inner recesses of his soul.

He then went home and threw himself face down on the floor before God in the agony of prayer.

"Oh God! Give me the life of my boys. Let me love them. Let me feed and provide for them. Let me give everything for them, and then, when they are old enough to look after themselves, then you can take them. Just give me time to love them now."

As he got up from the prayer, he knew he had touched God's heart. The contract has been signed and faith for the future rose in his heart.

The Welshman is my own Dad!

That's how I got all the inside details! The proof of answered prayer for the survival of his boys are the very lines of this book being written now! Both myself and my twin brother Colin survived, thanks to the intercessory prayer of our Dad. His prayer gives flesh to the rather misty, super-spiritual idea of intercession we sometimes have. He was willing to put everything he had into the prayer. To own it, possess it personally with love and sacrifice. And once possessing it, give it back to God, surrendering his own sovereignty in submission to God's best. This is the kind of intercession Jesus' life shows us. He owned the pain of suffering humanity, giving His all, His last drops of blood, to buy us back from death. He then gave it all back to God in faithful expectation of resurrection life. My Dad summed up another aspect of this prayer when he once shared with me.

"I went deep to the very depths. And there, at the very bottom, I touched a heart - the heart of God."

But the story doesn't end here. In fact, it is only just beginning!

As twin boys, we began our vulnerable journey into life. Nothing was ever said about the prayer and, apart from a couple of visits to Sunday School and learning the Lord's Prayer from Mum, we were not a churchgoing, religious family. I actually managed to say the whole prayer in under 10 seconds - adding to the time honoured liturgy, *"Bless me, Mum, Dad ,Colin, all my relations and all the people in the world,"* before the final *"Amen."*

Our first house was a little cottage in Old Welwyn with a yard, no bathroom and an outside loo. I used to love catching the mice in the mousetrap and then, holding them by the tail, ceremoniously flushing them down the loo. My brother was, at the same time, friend, enemy, constant companion and sparring partner.

Throughout childhood, my constant battle was with bronchitis. I could barely run without being reduced to breathless wheezing, and my early school years were punctuated by extended absences due to the illness. Some nights, I would wake up sweating, unable to breathe, wondering if I was going to die. However, thanks to much love and nursing, I pulled through.

After a short stay at Oxmoor Council Estate in Huntingdon, we moved to a new little house in Little Paxton, St Neots, which was to become our home for many years. I used to love going for walks with my Dad to the Gravel Pits which were not far away. What joy it was in winter to throw stones on the frozen lakes, hearing them resonate on the ice like some ethereal chorus. Sometimes, I would stay out deliberately in the rain just for the pleasure of feeling nearer to creation, nearer to God.

I had my fair share of childhood pranks. I remember one neighbour, Mrs Boswell, coming round one evening to complain,

"My Alan has lost all his eyebrows!"

Her Alan was my mate and we had found a box of matches. Unfortunately, we also found an old petrol drum in the woods. What a marvellous idea, I thought, to light a bit of paper, stuff it in the petrol drum, put the cap back on and run! I think my friend must have lost his eyebrows, whilst vainly trying to put the cap on, as the drum exploded into flames. I'd never heard of Molotov then, but that was my first and very last petrol bomb!

Although I was not a natural sportsman because of my health, I at least had perseverance. I loved rugby and from about twelve began to play in the school team. Regular matches and training gave me greater physical resilience and I seemed to grow out of the crippling effect of bronchitis. I had the joy of captaining our comprehensive school team to many victories and trophies. The comradeship, grit and team spirit, which the game gave me, have proved valuable assets, and the sheer physical outlet was also beneficial during the years of adolescence.

When I was growing up, I was known as *'fatty'* at school and then, when the beginnings of sport and adolescence had slimmed me down, I was known as *'spotty,'* because of the acne which signals, for so many, the rite of passage into manhood. I was often involved in fights because of this name-calling. I enjoyed study, was quite good and, backed up by an environment of love and acceptance at home, was able to progress on to 'O' and 'A' Levels. I got involved in drama and had the privilege of playing *'Mack The Knife'* in Brecht's *'Threepenny Opera'* and another role in Johnson's *'Bartholomew Fair'*. Getting up and acting in front of others enabled me to gain a certain confidence in public situations.

I was gifted more on the English Literature *'arty'* side than the scientific - much to the chagrin of my Dad who, for some strange reason, had it in his mind that his boys should become dentists! I've nothing against dentists, but I really couldn't envisage spending the rest of my life looking into people's mouths! In the end, we compromised and I finished up studying English, Maths and French. We were the first in our family to be able to go to University, my brother in London and myself in Norwich. University meant leaving home at eighteen and stepping into a whole new world.

My first roommate at University was a punk rocker known as "Switch," while my second was a committed, born-again Christian who later became a missionary in Chad. They both seemed to offer the extremes of choice that the freedom of University life offered.

During the Summer vacations, I worked as a courier on various campsites in France, a country to which I was beginning to feel more and more attracted. I was studying European Literature with a minor in the French Language which meant a year abroad in France. I taught English in two *'collèges'* in the lovely Breton town of Paimpol where I was placed as an *'assistant'*. I couldn't say that I learnt the French of 'Flaubert' as most of my language was picked up in the bars and football grounds, but I could at least communicate fairly fluently after that time.

I graduated and went to live in Finchley in North London where I thought I would spend a year doing odd jobs before launching into teacher training. I did not really have much ambition to teach but could not think of anything better at the time. I was secretly hoping that something else would appear during the year to give me some stronger direction. And something did appear, but not quite what I expected.

It all began when I received an unexpected telephone call from my Mum.

"Hello, Robert," she said.

"Your brother has gone all funny! He phoned up last night, saying that he's become a Christian. He said he loves us all and was happy."

I was flabbergasted. That was definitely not like my brother! I had kept up the contact with him during the University years. He had known his ups and downs and, at that time, was living in a squat opposite Millwall Football Ground, writing poetry and thinking about life.

The next day, he came to visit me. As he stood on the doorstep, beaming a smile at me, I couldn't help wondering if he had gone off his head and caught religious mania. It was worse when he said to me:

"You know Rob, the Holy Spirit now lives in me!"

"Oh no!" I thought.

"He's got into spiritualism."

I was genuinely uneasy and quite fearful of this new brother of mine who seemed to be on a different planet. I went on to the attack.

"Does that mean you don't swear anymore or go out with girls?" I exclaimed.

"I don't know about that," he replied. *"But I do know that I've met the love of Jesus. Before going on, you need to get to know more of Him. Have you read the Bible?"*

There he had me. In spite of my University education, I'd spent more time on Marx, Freud, Nietzsche and the French existentialists than on the founder of the Christian faith. I had to confess that I had never read much of the Bible. I suddenly realised what a gaping hole in my culture it was. I was still confident though.

"Ok, I'll read some of it and come back to you." I said, convinced by the commonly held idea that the Bible is full of contradictions and errors, only to be believed by the naive or the ignorant.

He left, promising to pray for me. As he walked away, I realised that he had something that I did not possess and, I knew deep down, that what he was saying about Jesus and redemption was true. I was just not ready to admit it to myself, or willing to pay the price of following Him.

In the days that followed, I read through the Gospels and the New Testament in a little Gideon's nurse's Bible that had unexpectedly turned up in the house. I was genuinely surprised and overwhelmed by the person of Jesus that the Gospels described. He was a million miles away from the *'gentle Jesus meek and mild'* image I had. He had courage, wisdom and the passionate love for humanity that was strong enough to change the world. I had always felt strongly about the sufferings and injustices of our earth and longed to be able to make a difference in some small way. I remember how crushed down I used to feel whilst watching *'News at Ten'*. With each 'bong' of Big Ben I would get more and more depressed.

Genocide in Cambodia - Bong!

Famine in Africa - Bong!

Another bomb in N. Ireland - Bong!

I longed to be able to change things, but felt powerless. I was living in Margaret Thatcher's constituency and battles were raging with the GLC, under the leadership of Ken Livingstone. I was delighted when tube fare prices went down, but enraged when they went up again under the Tories. Anger and frustration were building up and the ideas of Communism and violent rebellion were taking root. At the time, a group called *'Dexy's Midnight Runners'* had a song with the line,

"The only way to change things is to shoot men who arrange things," and, unconsciously, I was beginning to agree.

However, something new was challenging me as I got to know this person called Jesus through the Bible. His life of selfless integrity gave the lie to the selfish striving of so many, and His radical teaching about loving even our enemies was a level above anything else I had ever heard. And it was not just words. He modelled His own teaching, proving His love by dying alone on a cross and leaving this world with a lyric of forgiveness on His lips:

"Father, forgive."

Chairman Mao said that power was in the barrel of a gun, but I was coming to realise that true power lay in the apparent weakness of a crucified man on the cross - the power of love. The first brings power to destroy and crush, while the second defeats death and has the power of resurrection life. Truth was gradually dawning in my heart, but there was resistance.

A lot of my lifestyle in those days was in contradiction to that truth. Should I carry on in the comfort zone of living a lie, wearing the masks and trappings of a substandard life, or face the challenge of allowing a true, abundant life to take its place? A real civil war began in my heart. I was so drawn to Jesus and yet a powerful fear of radical change was holding me back.

My brother continued to visit me regularly and one day invited me to come to an evening they were organising at Goldsmith's College. Circumstances allowed for me to be free that evening and I found myself on a bus heading for Goldsmith's College in New Cross, South London. As I entered the college, an orchestra was rehearsing *'Belshazzar's Feast'* and little did I know that my own life was very much to be held in the balance that evening. As I walked into the meeting hall, I said to my brother:

"Don't think you'll get me to be a Christian tonight. I've got too much to lose!"

I'd never been to an evangelistic meeting before, so it was all new to me. Folks were friendly enough and the atmosphere relaxed. An evangelist called Andrew Page - he now works in Austria as a pastor, began to speak. The message was interspersed with two songs. The first was called, *'How much do you think you are worth boy?'* It unveiled the incredible value that God placed on each human life. Rather than see man perish, He paid for him with the blood of His own innocent Son. I realised that, even if I had been the only person alive in the world, Jesus valued me enough to come and give His life personally for me. In the battle that was raging within, truth was again asserting itself. The final lines of the song rang out -

"If it don't make you cry, laugh it off, pass it by, but remember the day when you threw it away, when he showed you how much you were worth!"

That clinched it. I couldn't pass by the truth that Jesus had died for me personally on the cross, and that such knowledge held me, in a strange way, responsible for my destiny. I'd vaguely heard about Jesus, the cross and sins before. I'd dismissed it all as dead religion, but now, a deep revelation of this historic - yet supernatural truth, was dawning in my heart.

"I can't deny it," I thought. *"But I can hide it."*

I quietly resolved to simply believe and be quiet. However, as I was feeling a bit relieved with this new solution, the singer started another song. He sung from the perspective of a man in the crowd who had to choose between Barabbas and Jesus. No half-measures! No neutral vote! You are either 100% for one or 100% for the other. No hiding in the middle! I was feeling challenged. It was as if I was the only person in the room and that God was speaking to me directly. The evangelist finished by saying that he was going to pray a prayer of commitment and that all those who wanted to give their lives to Jesus should simply pray AMEN at the end. The battle raged within me. Throughout his prayer, I had an inner voice within me saying:

"No! No! No! Don't say Amen. You've too much to lose."

The voice became more and more insistent as the prayer went on and I was pretty convinced that I was not going to step over the line of commitment. And then, suddenly, unexpectedly, another revelation eased itself sovereignly into my mind. It was like an inner vision. I had the impression of being confronted with a choice between eternal death or eternal life.

"Now is the time to choose," another voice said.

I had to make a decision and the power of the revelation made it an obvious choice - even if it meant losing all that I knew at the time. I said *"Amen"* and passed, with that simple affirmation, from death to life.

2 Caught up in the River

Several years ago, I went canoeing for the first time. I was a real beginner and volunteered to be the 'guinea pig' for some friends who were being examined for their instructor's award. Being on the bank was easy and I was quite enjoying waving my paddle around in the air. Getting in the canoe was a bit harder but, after a while, paddling around in the shallows was very pleasant. The water was still and there was no current. Everyone was having a wonderful time when suddenly the instructor cried out:

"Everyone over the weir now!"

I couldn't believe it! I had only volunteered to be 'dummy' and now I was getting caught up in the current, heading towards a roaring white-water weir! I was petrified. As the weir got closer, for some strange reason, my canoe would not go in a straight line and approached it sideways on. Suddenly, it was as if I was in the middle of a washing machine being rolled around in the rushing water. I emerged, paddle still in hand, but with the canoe merrily continuing on its way upside down. This provided the perfect opportunity for the instructors to demonstrate their rescue techniques as they got me back into the canoe. However, I could not get out of the current. There was no escape. The only way out was to go with the flow. I cannot remember how many times I capsized and was rescued before reaching the end. Other beginners were having the same problem.

I remember one Welsh girl, clinging for dear life to an overhanging tree, one foot in the canoe, the other on the bank. Another girl, after capsizing several times, abandoned canoe and paddle to the water and went walking off into the fields bordering the river. The whole thing was a nightmare! I had not mastered the basics of manoeuvring the canoe in order to enjoy the ride.

Years later, after many hours of practice, I was accomplished enough to be able to lead a team of canoeists down the 30 km of the very popular Ardèche river in France, enjoying every minute of negotiating the rapids and feeling the thrill of being in the current. These experiences proved to be a kind of living parable for my beginnings in walking with Jesus as a Christian. God catches us up in His ultimate purpose. His Spirit gives a new dynamic to lives that are shallow and in a rut. I know there have been many times when I have wanted out, or was simply in two minds before some situations - a very precarious position to take up, before deciding in the end to go with the current and try, with perseverance, to enjoy the experience.

My early Christian debuts were a bit of a nightmare. Up until then, most of my life had been built on values and practices that did not match up with the new life Christ offered. It was as if the little mustard seed of faith, which I had received that night at Goldsmith's College, was now moving the whole mountain of my past life and experience. It was not always a comfortable feeling. It often felt like a civil war was going on in my heart and I began to wonder who I really was. On one particular evening, I remember sitting down in front of the television to watch 'The Kenny Everett Video Show'. Normally I had no problem with such a programme but, as I sat on the sofa, something inside of me was uneasy to be watching some of the more compromising scenes. I could not believe it! Something very real and very radical had happened to me. I had never had a problem with sin until I discovered Jesus! As the days went by, more and more areas of my life were being challenged and I found myself on the verge of abandoning everything. The presence of this new life was far too uncomfortable and disabling for my usual lifestyle.

One morning, when I had more or less decided to pack it in, I received a letter from the evangelist who had preached the evening of my salvation. He strongly recommended that I try to find a church to go to. He gave me the name of an Anglican vicar in Finchley and let me know that he was praying for me. I was so ignorant about church life at that time. I hadn't ever considered that this 'becoming a Christian' was linked to going to church! It came as quite a shock to me, the idea of going to church, and I resolved that I would not do it. I had never been to a church since a couple of childhood visits to Sunday School, and I had even managed, in some strange way, to avoid marriages and funerals over the years.

A few days later, I was shopping in Tesco's, which was quite near where the church was. I had just bought some rhubarb and was heading homewards. Suddenly, I had a strong impression that I must go and see the aforementioned vicar. I ended up in front of the door of the vicarage. I rang the bell to be greeted, a few moments later, by the beaming face of Alfred Sawyer, an American vicar, who had come to serve the population of Golder's Green and beyond.

"Hi, Rob! Come on in!" he said.

"I've already heard about you."

I was a bit taken aback, but walked in. He was an incredibly open and friendly man, full of generosity and patience towards me. I explained some of the difficulties I was going through, and he encouraged me to come back on Sunday to take part in the Service. Although it had been a short visit, I felt strangely encouraged by it all.

Sunday arrived. I had never been to a proper Church Service before in my life, so I felt quite challenged. I arrived early and sat on a wooden park bench in front of St Paul's, North Finchley, listening to the church bell calling the faithful. The presence of God seemed so real to me at that moment, even though I was only just becoming aware of Him.

For someone who had never ever read or heard the Creeds - or even understood much about Church, I was quite touched by the Service and the message. However, I was still carrying quite an ache on the inside, struggling with the problems this new Christian life was bringing me.

After the Service, there was a 'Tear Fund' lunch given in aid of the poor of the world. It was all very nice, noble and the kind of thing you would expect from good Christian people, but deep within, I was still struggling to touch something real concerning Jesus. Was this it then? Had Jesus died on the cross and gone through all the agony for this? Was it worth it? Was it worth my own personal sacrifice of giving up the pleasures and security of sin for such a life?

"How are things going?" Alfred asked me.

"Well, I'm still not so sure," I replied.

He invited me back to the vicarage for a few moments of prayer with his wife and a parish worker. Little did I know it then, but those few moments of prayer were about to radically change the direction of my life.

Up until then, no one had ever spoken to me about the Holy Spirit. It seems that most people have no problem talking about God - even if their 'God' happens to be money, themselves or a plastic gnome in the garden! A more limited group may be free to talk about Jesus, but ask if anyone knows the Holy Spirit and you will probably be greeted with confused silence. God, the Father, okay, God the Son, just about, but God the Holy Spirit remains a mystery to many. And yet, it is the Holy Spirit who makes Jesus real to us. Without the dynamic relationship with the Holy Spirit, Jesus remains a mere historical figure, a kind of 'holy hippie' walking the streets of Galilee in sandaled feet and yet irrelevant to the world of twenty-first century men. The Holy Spirit puts Jesus into your flesh!

Anyway, in blissful ignorance of any theology and with only a beginner's grasp of the Bible, I took my place in the vicarage, sitting a couple of metres away from the others. I was deeply aware of my own need.

"Let's pray!" Alfred said.

Apart from my hurried *'Lord's Prayer'* - which I had long since abandoned, I had never vocalised prayer before. What on earth could I pray?

Out of the very depths of me, the only thing that would come out without sounding false, embroidered or hypocritical, were the words,

"Help me!"

"God, help me!" I prayed.

I was not expecting anything to happen, so I was all the more surprised when a kind of shiver seemed to wash over me. The shiver was followed by a wave of love, which seemed to break almost physically over me. Another wave and another, each coming with greater force, bringing a warm supernatural encouragement of God's presence. I had never known anything like it. It was quite supernatural, spiritual and yet physical.

Amazing! I felt as though I was going to burst inside and, when a more intense wave rushed over me, my heart seemed to explode and I began to weep with tears of healing and inexpressible joy. Alfred and the others also seemed to be enjoying the same glorious experience of God.

"God has met with you," they said.

"You've experienced the filling of the Holy Spirit."

I was quite overwhelmed. It was as if I had stepped into a kind of spiritual elevator which had taken me far above my problems. Of course, my problems were still there, but I had received a completely different perspective on them. Instead of being under them, I was far above.

"God has taken the 'fag end' of your life and given you, in exchange, a beautiful palace," someone said.

I knew that I had received something special from God. I was filled with a real love and knew inside that I belonged forever to God. I left the house a new man. I had been caught up in a powerful current of love and my own heart was also overflowing with the joy of knowing Jesus. As I walked in the streets of Finchley, I had an indescribable - yet genuine, love for the complete strangers around me. It was as if my little human heart had been suddenly invaded by the immense love of the Father. I could hardly hold it in! I walked down Long Lane and made my way to the tube station. As I bought my ticket, I could no longer restrain myself and I leant over and hugged the lady who had just sold me the ticket saying,

"Jesus really loves you!"

She must have thought I was mad.

When I got home, I found my little Gideon's Bible. There at the back was a blank space entitled *'My Decision'.* Before, I had not had the conviction to fill it in for fear of giving up later, but now I was absolutely convinced. I signed my name.

God had taken up residence.

3 Called

Cigarette packets carry Government health warnings and, in a more positive way, the receiving of the Holy Spirit should also have its own warning. Far from being merely the calling card for membership of the happy, clappy Christian club, the Holy Spirit, the Spirit of Jesus, turned my life upside-down in the same radical way that Jesus turned over the tables of the money changers and chased out the robbers from His Father's temple. If you want the Holy Spirit to come, be prepared for change.

All of the changes were for the better. Over the years, I had picked up the habit of swearing profusely. I asked the Lord to help me with this, and within weeks I no longer swore. I longed to share my experiences with others. I felt no embarrassment in doing so, and it seemed so natural to share my faith with people. In the early weeks of my conversion, I spoke to literally hundreds of people about what had happened to me. Through my work I met elderly people, handicapped folk and working men. I learned much from them all and found that most people were interested in hearing about Jesus. My brother was overjoyed to hear of all that had happened and he used to invite me to stay with a Christian friend in Birmingham where we were both very much encouraged. I loved reading the Bible and I became a regular member of St Paul's, Finchley, where Alfred, the vicar, was a faithful listener and encourager.

Before long, my brother sent me some information concerning a dynamic group of young people who used to take teams of Christians to foreign lands. The idea of travel had always interested me, so I wrote away for information concerning their Summer activities to North Africa. I received a very warm response to my letter and felt attracted to this group, although I had very little idea of what they were about. Along with my brother, Colin, we decided to spend a weekend with them at their base in South

Wales, Llanelli.

The weekend was very special. There were a whole group of us, many who were later to form the nucleus of the future work of this mission, with lots of laughs and lots of enthusiasm for the work of the Gospel. One young man who was already working full-time for the group took up a guitar. He had a particular ministry through song. As he sung, I clearly saw Jesus in him. It was strange, but it seemed to be a confirmation of His presence within this band of young, inexperienced pioneers. An older man, wise with prayer, led the group – we were twenty people at the time. He did not say much, did not push himself forward, but a quiet authority seemed to come from him.

I arrived back in London, convinced that I should be joining these folks on a trip to North Africa. I was intrigued by the lifestyle of this group where trust in Jesus seemed to be so vital. They all lived by faith which meant counting on the Lord - and in real terms friends, family and church groups, rather than on a regular salary to live. Prayer and vision for the unreached people groups of the world who had no Christian tradition or heritage – who remained totally outside of the scope of the Gospel, seemed to animate them strongly. I was still, however, very much a learner, and I think I was more attracted by the spirit of adventure than by any real grasp of missionary endeavour. At the time, I had not really understood that this work was in fact a new missionary movement and had associated it more with a Christian holiday ministry.

As I was working for Barnet County Council, I needed to finish my job in order to go to North Africa. I resigned and had a couple of days to make preparations and buy the relevant equipment necessary for the North Africa expedition. We would be sleeping outside, so I quickly bought a cheap sleeping bag and threw a few old clothes into a rucksack. The next day, I turned up at *The Good Shepherd Mission* in 3 Colts Lane, Whitechapel, which was the rendezvous point for the thirty of us going. A very mixed bunch arrived.

After a cup of tea, we all sat down in a circle and introduced ourselves. The experienced man, who was leading the trip, asked everyone to give his or her reasons for going on the expedition. Various ones began to share. Several talked of a burden they were carrying for North Africa. I was still very unfamiliar with Christian jargon so I wondered if they would be carrying extra large rucksacks or something! Others mentioned that they may be called to the Arab world. It then came to my turn to share. Wanting to be as honest as possible, I simply confessed:

"Well, I'm looking to have a jolly good holiday!"

There was an embarrassed silence and then a number burst out laughing. When the laughter stopped, the leader looked over to me and said in his sober Welsh accent:

"It certainly won't be a holiday."

I felt really stupid, and yet at the same time, convicted inside that this was indeed going to be much more than a holiday for me. It wasn't the last time either that I was to be convicted by the wise words of this Welsh apostle.

My hippie length hair was also out of place in the group - and probably unsuitable for creating a good image in North Africa, so I allowed one of the ladies on the team to cut it back to more acceptable proportions. As the locks fell to the floor, I wondered what rite of passage was being enacted? This ritual was launching me into a new world and lifestyle.

We arose early the next day and set off in two old Ford Transit minibuses known as HKK and DBL after their last letters on the number plates. We could not go very fast so it took ages to get to the Ferry Port. I had almost had enough after only three hours, so I was beginning to dread the three day non-stop drive which was ahead of us through France, Spain and into Africa!

We made the ferry, and whilst we were relaxing in the lounge of the boat, the leader called us together for a meeting. He began to explain about the situation for those who convert to Christ in some Arab states.

"Many undergo severe persecution from friends, family and society if they turn to Christ. They may well lose their jobs, their friends, and, in some extreme cases, their very life, through being poisoned or knifed."

He looked up and challenged us:

"Your message of Jesus has to be more than words. What would you do if that believer came to you with his problems? Could you say, 'Here, have my job for your lost one. I'll come and live with you and be your friend?' And ultimately, could you say, 'Here, give me the poison, I'm willing to die in your place?"

We were all strangely silent afterwards. My 'holiday' idea was dying a death and I wondered what I had gotten myself into. If we had not been in the middle of the Channel, I would probably have gone home.

Dietrich Bonhoeffer, the German theologian who died for his faith in a concentration camp, said:

"When Christ calls a man, He bids him, "Come and die."

At the very beginning of my Christian adventure, I was beginning to overhear this solemn, yet strangely enticing, invitation.

It was not easy being in such close confinement with so many people. The Christian veneer of niceness soon wore off after the first thousand kilometres of cramped conditions, and, despite the prayer and holy words, each one was confronted with the reality of the other. Try maintaining close fellowship with a travelling companion who has not washed or changed his socks for four days!

As we travelled from Algeciras via the Straits of Gibraltar to Ceuta, the gateway to Africa, excitement was beginning to mount. North Africa greeted us with its mosques, markets, calls to prayer and mosquitoes! Everything was so new and different. I felt strangely vulnerable in the midst of such a society. As we walked the streets praying, or playing football on the beaches, we were able to make friends and naturally share our faith in Christ.

Over the next three weeks, we travelled further south where we were able to help in the establishment of a future work. Our older mentor taught and modelled prayer. He also introduced the practice of Biblical meditation to help each of us hear God for himself. Those lessons of prayer and meditation have served me in good stead ever since. I was still a very young Christian and found much of the expedition difficult. I got frustrated with the other folks and would go off with my brother, Colin, to criticise and judge everything and everyone! Most of the group went down with some stomach bug - commonly known as 'the lergy', and it was a regular sight to see folk nipping off into the bush, shovel in one hand, Izal loo roll in the other. I did wonder whether the choice of the greaseproof, harsh, Izal paper had more to do with trying to create a sense of monastic hardship than simple economic realities! I later counted my blessings when I learned that the local population have to be content with using a stone - a rounded one I hasten to add! One particular shy guy would walk miles to find a secluded spot, but inevitably ended up perched on the top of a distant hill in full view of everyone! We nicknamed him *'the Izal man.'*

At one point, the team divided into mini-expedition groups. Our group had decided to climb up Mount Toubkal and pray. It sounded very exciting, but I do not think any of us had quite grasped the reality that Mount Toubkal is about as high as Mont Blanc and quite a difficult trek. My brother, Colin, was with me in the group. So, armed with my cheap sleeping bag, sun hat and a pair of plimsolls, I set off. It really was a long, hard climb, and yet there were magnificent views. After climbing all day in the heat, we were only about halfway up. We would need to camp out on the mountain. It had been so hot during the day but now, as night fell, it became quite cold and a roaring wind began to blow. In an effort to survive the cold, I proposed that my brother and I join our sleeping bags together in order to sleep closer and generate more warmth. The idea was good in theory, but what I had not planned on, was the fact that my brother had another way of generating warmth! As we were neatly nestled together, like sardines in a tin - the top of the sleeping bag closed over us, I realised that my brother had stomach problems. The wind was blowing outside, but another less generous wind was also very much blowing inside. I was getting ratty.

"Look, Colin," I said. *"If you do that again, I'll punch you on the nose!"*

He shouted back at me, complaining that my elbow was in his ear. We were still young Christians so our language had not quite the sanctified edge expected from those on apostolic journeys. Finally, I had had enough, and landed a punch on him. He punched back and we ended up having a fight. It was all over in five minutes. As twins, we'd had twenty-three years practice of fighting together so it was no big deal and we settled back to finally sleep. However, the next morning the rest of the team was a bit worried.

"Are you okay?" they asked.

Fistfights were not the 'done' thing on prayer expeditions!

We finally reached the top and were able to spend time praying and proclaiming Christ's Lordship over Africa from a high point in that land. As the expedition went on, it was as if the worst parts of me were expressing themselves, but, in spite of that, I was also discovering a seed of God's grace, which was starting to sprout, filling me with the beginnings of Christ's love and compassion for people.

One evening, we found ourselves celebrating an Arab wedding in a little village. I looked around at the beautiful girls who were singing and dancing. They were about twelve-years-old. Usually, when you look into the eyes of a twelve-year-old child you see a kind of inner light of innocence which you hope the world has not yet succeeded in smothering. However, as I looked into the eyes, all I could see was a kind of darkness. A dark religion held them in its cold grip. What hope did this loveless religion bring to them? I was deeply challenged inside of me. Who could bring the light of Jesus to such sad eyes? I could feel a struggle going on inside of me. Could God really be asking me, ordinary, rebellious me, to be available to serve Him? I had never before contemplated missionary work and felt daunted even with the thought of it. It was a different world! But now this world was becoming my reality.

On the long journey back, I had time to think and chat it over with the others. Some had found the discipline of the trip and the no frills leadership a bit hard to take and tried to discourage me. However, something was nagging away inside which would not leave me in peace.

When we arrived in France, I thought I may well have resisted the niggle and would soon be home, back in the old routine which was guaranteed to deaden the challenging inner voice which was so uncomfortable. However, I wasn't counting on breaking down in Poitiers! Poitiers is well known as the place where Charles Martel fought a decisive battle which pushed Arab invaders back out of Europe. It is less known as the place where God decided to meet with me and call me to His service.

Our minibus started emitting masses of white smoke on the motorway outskirts of Poitiers and we managed to pull in at a garage. A number of folks crushed into the second bus to continue the journey home whilst five of us volunteered to wait with the bus until the vital spare part could be delivered from Wales. As you might imagine, there is not a lot of stimulating activity going on at most '*Autoroute*' garages, so I had lots of time on my hands to be able to pray and read the Bible.

Early one morning, as the sun was rising, I was meditating on Paul's words in 2 Corinthians 2 vs. 14-16:

"But thanks be to God, who always leads us in triumphal procession in Christ and through us spreads everywhere the fragrance of the knowledge of him. For we are to God the aroma of Christ among those who are being saved and those who are perishing. To the one we are the smell of death; to the other, the fragrance of life. And who is equal to such a task?"

As I read, the words seemed to be writing themselves onto my very heart and I felt a strange warmth, as the Holy Spirit himself seemed to be re-breathing those same words in a personal message to me at that moment. God was calling me to follow Jesus in triumphant procession. He was asking me to be the 'perfume of God' in this world. I could feel my heart beating, sensing that this was indeed a call from God as He spoke to my spirit. I felt so unequal to the task, and yet faith was dispelling the fear and I so wanted to say yes. Later that morning, I went to see the team leader to tell him my experience and ask if he would be willing to take on somebody as 'green' as myself within their growing mission. He said he would pray about it, but gave me the necessary encouragement I needed to press on.

"Please phone us up in a couple of week's time and we'll let you know whether you can come," he said.

The desire to serve God did not fade away as I settled back into life in London. Alfred Sawyer, my vicar, was very positive about a move into mission with this group and I was overjoyed when the leader and the others in the mission team in Llanelli said that they were willing to take me on. I gave in my notice on the flat I was renting, managed to get all my possessions into one big blue sack and made my way to Paddington Station to take a train to Wales - and a whole new life. No salary, no job security, just an overriding conviction that God would honour His word and His call.

At the same time, my brother Colin received his own call to invest his life within the *'Icthus'* movement of churches in South East London and he joined their training programme.

I dropped in on my Dad and Mum before leaving. Dad had been a bit worried about both his boys giving up the possibility of lucrative careers for the instability of Christian work. However, before leaving, his worry changed to a quiet satisfaction as he told me, for the first time, how he had prayed as a young boy in the Dr Barnardo's home all those many years back.

"I think I'm beginning to understand now," he said.

"Rather than letting you die and take you to himself when you were born, God has given me the privilege of looking after you, but is now taking you back again to Himself in your new birth. Not in death now – but as a living sacrifice, a consecrated life. Yes, I think I'm beginning to understand! Well, I never! I thought God had forgotten!"

God doesn't forget our intercessory prayers. As I was on the train, heading back to the land of Wales where the prayer had begun all those many years ago, I felt such a peace and joy, knowing that I was walking steadfastly into my own personal destiny - a joyful victim of intercession's love.

4 New Horizons

Coming from the South of England, Llanelli seemed as foreign a place as I had ever been to. Little did I understand the great spiritual heritage Wales possessed. Not far from Llanelli, the famous revivalist Evan Roberts had prayed for 100,000 souls to be saved at the turn of the 20th Century. His prayer ushered in the great Welsh Revival of 1904 when the Holy Spirit brought the thousands Roberts had prayed for into the Kingdom of God. Hundreds of stern, square chapels littered the towns and villages of Wales in memory of those heady days of God's presence when each one would have been full to overflowing.

Another Welshman, Rees Howells, had been caught up in the 'fire' of the Revival and found God using him in remarkable ways through his intercessory prayers. This coal miner became a 'prince of prayer', and was mightily used to establish the Bible College of Wales in Swansea, which in turn became a 'House of Prayer for All Nations', helping shape the destiny of many countries and playing a key intercessory role during the Second World War. Norman Grubb's book, *'Intercessor'*, gives an account of Rees Howell's life and is a challenging, life-changing read for anyone willing to learn more about the power of prayer and obedience to God.

The leader of the North African trip, another Welshman from near Swansea, and founder of the mission that I was joining, seemed to have his roots in this same rich soil. Coming out of a difficult background of spiritualism and fraudulent car deals, he found himself serving as a soldier in Malaysia. During this time, he contracted cerebral malaria, and lay dying in hospital. In some sovereign expression of grace, the Lord met with him while he was in the hospital.

Over a period of time, the Lord revealed himself through a number of channels - a man singing a hymn, a growing sense of God. All of this came to a head while reading a novel by Nevil Shute, *Round the Bend*, about a man who founded a new religion. The last sentences of the book contained the simple statement.

"I have walked and talked with God."

This phrase seemed to penetrate deep and confirm something of the quiet presence of God in a heart seeking after truth. It was also to become an intercessory 'leitmotiv' for the rest of his life.

After this process of faith, he found himself miraculously healed from his malaria and rejoined his army comrades a changed man. He was no longer attracted to violence and bawdy parties. He found himself physically unable to drink the beer he would have downed with relish a few months earlier!

"What on earth has happened to me?" he asked a friend on the boat returning to Britain.

"It seems to me you've become a Christian. You've been born again!" replied the friend, praying for him and giving a kind of formal recognition to a Christian birth which had probably been conceived back in the hidden destinies of the prayers of the Welsh Revival.

This Welshman's heart's desire from that time on was to be able to serve God as a missionary - preferably back amongst the peoples of Malaysia. He served for many years in a couple of mission agencies, developing his love and practice of prolonged periods of prayer and Bible study, as well as being strongly involved in inner-city outreach to the poor and destitute. He married a lovely wife and the Lord blessed them with a little girl.

In the early 70's, the church in Britain was experiencing a breath of renewal and many new church groups were forming. This Welsh intercessor became a very popular itinerant Bible teacher for such gatherings. As he was at the height of his ministry and in much demand, the Lord challenged him to consecrate the next years of his life to total prayer and, in doing so, to pull out of public life. A burden of intercession seemed to descend on his heart as dew might cover an awaiting earth. The days came and went in prayer. Days became weeks, weeks months and months years. The Lord was leading him to a prolonged period of intercession. After three years of intense prayer - followed by two more years, the burden seemed to gently lift. Five years of prayer! I remember asking him how he managed to pray for that long. What did he pray? Did he have a long list of subjects? His answer surprised me.

"You know," he said,

"Intercession is like your heart is breaking. It's a sharing in Jesus' crying out for the nations of the world. Sometimes a prayer is simply expressing the inner longings of Jesus for a world of people. I can sum up the prayer God gave me in one sentence:

'O God! Give me your work to do!'

Sometimes I could verbalise all of it. Sometimes the burden would be so much that I could only cry out, 'Oh God', and sometimes, all I could do was throw myself face down on the mountain heights in God's presence."

During this time, God built into his servant some of the faith principles which were to be vital in the birthing and discipling of a mission movement. At one time, the Lord led him not to receive any gifts other than those whose source was unknown. In order to survive, he pawned precious war medals and got down to possessing only his clothes and a suitcase with another change of clothes.

"Well Lord, there it is. We can't really go much further now. Even if it means dying and starving, we will still follow."

The breakthrough came. They survived the testing of faith and the Lord seemed to whisper, as he had whispered similarly to Abraham of old,

"Because you have been faithful in this, you can now reach out at any time into my treasury."

What a promise! It has been this foundation of faith that has since released hundreds of workers and millions of pounds into world mission.

After the five years of prayer, this praying family were led to Llanelli where they decided to do something for the town by initiating outward-bound activities for the local young people who used to hang around with nothing to do. Canoeing on a lake in the aptly named *'Swiss Valley'*, mountain walks and plaggy-bagging - sliding down snow-covered hills on a bin liner for the uninitiated, made up some of the activities. As the young people came, the natural continuation of the fun was a small gathering of folk around the Bible.

An anointing from heaven seemed to descend on the region. God had answered the years of intercession and many young people began finding the Lord. Children would pray in the schools and whole classes got converted. Many churches in the region were able to develop youth groups, which seemed to grow and grow. As the locality was being blessed, our Welsh apostle seemed to hear the Lord speak to him again.

"I want you to take some of these young people to the nations."

At first, the idea was simply to give them some basic discipling and vision and then, for those with a genuine call, send them to a more established mission agency. After a trip to France, where an American mission leader had strongly challenged him about setting up his own structures for sending missionaries, and a chance meeting with another man of similar vision, the scene was set for a tentative start up of a visible identity for the youth group. It was a vulnerable beginning. A communist man lent a hall for some of the early meetings and the willing young students, who had come for an activity weekend, found themselves sharing the same floor that dogs had obviously used previously in their own show!

One of the first vehicles was a rusty VW van, which had been found in two halves on the scrap heap. After welding it together, it became one of the first expedition vehicles. Apart from the local outward-bound activities, which were still proving popular, a few ventured overseas to France and Italy, twinning outdoor activities with prayer and evangelistic literature distribution. As more sturdy vehicles were acquired, the expeditions went further, going through France and Spain into the desert lands of North Africa.

After such trips and expeditions, a few of the young students felt an irresistible tug of the Holy Spirit to come and work alongside this Welsh pioneer in Llanelli. The first candidates were innocent and dynamic with a clear sense of calling and Kingdom purpose - young misfits when joining, but later to became key leaders, carrying God's anointed ministry to many nations of the world.

I joined with a whole batch of new folk at the time when Glanmor - the first building, had been purchased. As I approached Glanmor for the first time, a small group were just leaving for France in a small VW Beetle. It was the tentative launching of a work in this land. Little did I know it then, how much France was to play a leading role in my life in the future.

As soon as I arrived, I was given a job - scraping the stairs. Even after thirty years of ministry, I'm still scraping and cleaning things. The only change is that I'm scraping the walls of a big white Chateau now! Still, that's a later story. The hours passed. No one seemed to let me know when it was lunchtime, or teatime! After a few more hours of scraping, I retired, hungry, to Number 9, the boys' house where I had a room. Actually, it was a kind of attic with no heating and a roof window which blew off in high winds, exposing me to the elements! If anything, it was good training for camping out on the Black Mountains!

We were five single men living in the house and none of us had much idea about how to live normally! As tired faces used to emerge hungrily in the morning, rush downstairs, grab whatever food was available and then run off, I used to think about the early cavemen, struggling for survival in a fight of the fittest.

The house really did resemble a cross between the black hole of Calcutta and a London doss house. Milk bottles, unwashed and unreturned for months, would line the stairs in a kind of fungus offering to some unknown God! One fellow who came to stay with us said that walking up the stairs was like walking on the moon as all the dust would rise up at each step. Going to the loo was in itself a step of faith. Half of the loo was already poking through the downstairs ceiling and each time you took your place for a comfortable moment of mediation, it was wise to grip the chain tightly in case you found yourself abseiling down the lounge wall with your trousers round your ankles! We tried our best at home improvements. One attempt at putting in hot water left one guy with singed fingers and me with my slippers on fire!

Looking back, I am sure the physical mess reflected the way our inner lives were in the same kind of shambles, and the fear and passivity which held us back from making a difference. Happily, Number 9 has since been totally renovated - as has the whole of the rundown station area where it was located. I wonder if I can say the same concerning my own spiritual life?

In spite of the material hardship, I enjoyed my time immensely. I was young and untouched by religious cynicism, full of hope concerning my future with Jesus, and overwhelmed by a sense of privilege at being able to serve Him - even if I didn't know when dinner was being served!

I thrived in the environment of buoyant faith, communal work and Spartan conditions. Whole days were given over to praying together for the different nations of the world. We were all very green and unprepared but, as we prayed, we would find faith rising which transcended the reality of our youth and inexperience. Often we would open out maps of various countries and pray for them.

One dear friend - a red headed man from Cornwall, would often stand up in meetings, presenting himself as *The West African Team*. It seemed ridiculous at the time, but through much faith and perseverance, several expeditions - many of which strategically broke down in the middle of the Sahara, and a lot of prayer, he managed to pioneer a new work into the desert stronghold of Niger and establish bases all over Western Africa. There is now a very strong indigenous team. I remember him and some other key bodies being inspired to pray over a map of Northern Africa. As we prayed, there was an impression that the Lord wanted to lead us into the immeasurably more of faith that we hardly dared dream or hope for. Tentatively at first, a few began to pray for the establishment of prayer/training bases within some of the most resistant countries to the Gospel. Others took up the prayer with more conviction until we were almost praying out prophetically what the Lord had in mind.

"O God! We are asking you to ring the Sahara with prayer bases!"

The prayer would have been stupid and presumptuous had it not been inspired by a kind of outrageous faith which gripped our young hearts. Years later, as I write today, the Lord has led us to just about complete the task, as we have gone and pioneered bases in places where folk told us it was impossible. One day, I hope that many stories will be written by the pioneers who made such progress possible.

As well as learning about prayer, there was also a strong emphasis on learning to hear God. As God speaks mainly through His written word, we were introduced to the concept of Biblical meditation. Spending quality time digesting short passages of God's word and allowing it to speak personally to the heart. Morning by morning, we would meet together, sharing the fruits and encouragements we had gleaned from God's word.

At the same time, I had been challenged by a book written by a man called Ralph Shallis - *'From Now On'*, who was a missionary in France. He felt it normal to give back to God at least a tithe of our time in prayer and meditation. That makes approximately two and a half-hours a day. This time was to be added to the normal workday and church duties. He also proposed the reading through of the entire Bible at least once a year. Year after year, the systematic overview and grip would build up. These have been principles that I have tried to keep up - thanks more to God's grace than any particular attribute on my part, and which have formed the bedrock of any ministry the Lord has sought to develop through me.

I was also learning the very practical art of living by faith - or praying in money to live on. Much to the chagrin of friends and family, our mission paid no wages. Quite the opposite in fact! Each one was responsible for supporting his own needs - rent and food, plus the costs of his ministry, including all expenses for travel. Apart from the very practical things folk needed to do - like getting sent out from the church, putting out an information letter for friends and family, the emphasis was placed on the ability to trust God and pray in finances in the manner of the early faith mission pioneers like George Muller of Bristol and Hudson Taylor, who founded the China Inland Mission.

One of my biggest barriers to overcome was independence and pride. Why should I depend on others to meet my needs? To make it worse, my mother told me how difficult she found it to explain to friends what I was involved in.

"Those boys of yours who went to University, what are they doing now?" Neighbours would ask.

"Well, some kind of missionary work," came the sheepish reply.

"Oh, and how much do they earn?"

"Well, actually, nothing. They are supported by friends and churches."

"Oh! I could never do that - it's like begging!"

And there it was. The terrible inner accusation of sponging off others! As I thought about it, I found that the condemnation did not come from God, but rather from a prevailing world attitude that opposes anything that goes against the grain. As I read the Bible, I could see that even Jesus, God Incarnate, in whom were hidden all the treasures of wisdom, humbled himself to receive help from others. He received meals from friends and was even helped financially by the women in his team - see the Gospel of Luke, Chapter 8 Verse 3. His dependency was their opportunity. My proud independence and shame was only closing the door of opportunity on others.

At that time, I had not even one penny of support from anyone so I was hardly giving much opportunity anyway! The Lord led me to give away what savings I had amassed, leaving me with just £50 which was a birthday gift. At a meeting one night, I heard of a colleague in France who needed £50 for a language course. The Lord prompted me to meet that need and, without thinking or questioning it, I gave the money away. The next day, I received a telephone call from my mother saying that I had just won £50 on the Premium Bonds. God works in mysterious ways!

Another test in the early days, was a couple of weeks away working on promotion at the annual Spring Harvest event. We tried to make our stand a bit more animated and aggressive than the average missionary stand. I ended up dressing as a Frenchman and, armed with an over the top accent, striped jumper and onions, would accost passers-by, challenging them to an onion-eating contest. Other mad antics included abseiling up the carpet and setting up an Arab Kasbah. All in the cause of recruiting workers for mission of course!

Whilst I was away, I realised that I would be needing about £100 to cover the various expenses of the event. I had nothing, and no expectation or inkling of where any money could come from. On returning home, I found two letters in the post from folks who were totally unaware of any such need. Both contained cheques for £50. As I opened the letters, I clearly felt God giving me much more than just £100. He was building up my faith and letting me know that I really could trust Him for finances.

I don't know whether the French beret had some kind of osmotic effect on me, but as I pranced about as 'Gaston de Cornichon', endeavouring to kiss as many attractive ladies as possible with the traditional French greeting, I felt a growing intuition that perhaps the Lord may be asking me to go to France. To test out the calling, I volunteered to help lead the French teams that year down in Sorgues, near Avignon, in the South of France.

A less favourable revelation from this 'Spring Harvest' time was the fact that I had picked up an illness. As I drove home, huge spots began appearing all over me. Within two days, I was totally covered and deformed by the spots which rapidly became itchy scabs. I had caught chicken pox. The temptation was to feel sorry for myself and sink into a pit of discouragement. As I lay in my sleeping bag in the humid attic room, I was indeed tempted to give it all up. I opened a letter that a friend had sent me from London. All that was inside was a postcard of a big sunflower and a prophetic word that the person had felt led to send:

"Take courage, little flower, you will come through."

I had never thought of myself in terms of a flower, but as I read the words, tears welled in my eyes, and I felt the warm glow of God's love and encouragement strengthening my heart. After a few weeks, the scabs began falling off, leaving their scars. The illness had been a testing time, but I had come through. It was as if the scabbiness of my old sinful life was being shorn away in brokenness, leaving scars, yes, but also revealing the potential of a life filled with the Spirit of Jesus.

I used to be responsible for corresponding with our folks in North Africa and, in the early days, I learnt to type - although I probably had more *'Tippex'* than type on the average letter. I also gave myself to developing a multi-media presentation of mission, using drama and slides of various nations. This meant that I was away most weekends with a small team doing promotions in various churches. I used to really love being away. Firstly, because it gave me the opportunity to stay in someone's warm house, sit on comfortable chairs and eat good food! It was also an opportunity of learning to share publicly in meetings.

On returning from one such trip, I went upstairs to my room, longing to throw myself on the bed and sleep. Unfortunately, the attic window had blown in during my absence, leaving a weekend's worth of rain on my bed! At the same moment, a friend in the house knocked on the door and came in looking a bit embarrassed.

"I'm sorry to disturb you Rob," he said. *"But I've got to pay the rent now. I know that you've kept up your payments, but some of the others haven't and we're £20 short. You wouldn't have £20 to give me would you?"*

You can probably imagine the kind of self-righteous, angry, frustrated emotions which began rising in me when I heard that. I had in fact just received £20 that weekend, so I was also trying on the inside to give a million and one reasons why I shouldn't give it. However, when the initial reaction died down, leaving space for me to hear the gentle whisper of the Holy Spirit, I felt he was actually prompting me to lay aside my own needs and problems, lay aside my sense of injustice at paying for what others had not paid - hadn't He paid my unjust debt on the cross, and hand over the £20. At first it was hard, but, as I did it, I felt an inner freedom and joy. He had conquered once again!

Within the mission, it was usual practice to encourage each person's home church to send them out. I had been grateful to Alfred Sawyer - the vicar, and the congregation at St Paul's and St Luke's in North Finchley for all the encouragement they had given me as I came to the Lord, but I had never thought about the need to be sent out by them. Alfred was open to the idea and a few of us planned to travel to London from Llanelli to present our mission to the church. As we were driving up the M4, another one of the senior leaders in the mission, turned to me and asked,

"Is your church Evangelical?"

"What's Evangelical?" I replied, in total ignorance.

After a worried glance back at me, he carried on driving.

Only a few people turned up for the Service, but it did build a solid link back to the church which has been faithful in prayer and support over the years. I feel such a depth of gratitude to so many ordinary folk who have prayed for us over the years from this Anglican Church. Noble, ordinary families who, in spite of their own challenges in life, always found space to welcome and care for us, giving time and money to support and promote our ministry.

As I prayed for the service, the Lord seemed to share with me a word from 1 Chronicles 29 v 1:

"The one whom God has chosen is young and inexperienced. The task is great because this palatial structure is not for man but for the Lord God."

Little did I realise then, how considerable the work was to be and how much building of temples the future held. All I could see was my youth and inexperience.

5 Destination France

"Sur le pont d'Avignon, on y danse, on y danse, sur le pont d'Avignon, on y danse tout en rond."

So goes the well-known French song.   And 'Avignon' was indeed the destination of our French Summer teams.

The entry into France had been pioneered by Claire Armstrong from Llanelli and another godly lady who used to work in a Christian bookshop near Valence.   They had linked with a faithful American missionary called Pansy Wright who had known and worked with our Welsh leader for several years - they had almost launched a mission centre in the Savoie region together.   She had gotten to know him when he had been the driver and prayer warrior for Yan Jones from the Bible College of Wales.   He had made several teaching visits to France, through the North and South East, and had been able to pray over the land.   The Ardèche region had also been visited for canoeing camps at the Pont d'Arc.

The work eventually moved, with a growing team, to a town near Avignon, called Sorgues, to link with a humble, faithful and courageous British couple - Maurice and Fiona, who were pioneering a church in the town.   They had links with our Welsh leader which went back to his time of prayer in the Birmingham area.   This powerful prayer warrior had long had a burden to work in France and even began to learn the language.   Each time, however, that he was to make a venture into the land, the Lord seemed to call him back.   On two occasions this was due to the death of one of his parents on the eve of both trips.   He would always keep a few French francs on him in the hope that he would be ready should the Lord open the door to this land again.   One day, a young man was speaking about his work in France and he felt the Lord asking him to lay down his own hopes for France by giving over his last francs to the man.   He obeyed and the seed was sown into the ground to die.

As I headed towards Avignon, I couldn't help feeling that my own life was somehow carrying the investment of those francs and that, in some strange way, I was taking up the baton that had been lain down in sacrificial worship all those years back. I felt privileged to be stepping onto the foundation of prayer that had been sown years earlier. Incredibly, we had four tyre blowouts on the journey, only to break down near Valence. Thankfully, we were able to repair the vehicle after yet another overnight stay camping out on a French Autoroute lay-by.

Our base in Sorgues was a Catholic school, where we were also to rendezvous with a group of French and Swiss Christians on their way to North Africa. I enjoyed chatting in French to one particular Swiss lady called Sylviane and, as she left for North Africa asking God whether He was calling her to serve Him with the mission, I wondered if we would meet up again.

Maurice and Fiona were very welcoming and became a real 'Mum' and 'Dad' to the tiny work which was developing. Their church provided the right kind of cover and base for the evangelistic outreach. Maurice was also an excellent teacher, not only of the French language itself, but also of the culture and sociology of France, which was so important to grasp.

As a team, we were able to learn a few French choruses and a few mimes and dramas. Avignon in the Summer has a big festival with many buskers, theatre groups, weird sects, fortune tellers and all sorts of extroverts doing their thing in the big *"Palais des Papes"* square, dominated by the immense statue of the Virgin Mary. We were able to take our place amongst them and present the Gospel through music, mime, testimony and word. Lots of people would gather around, many of them outside the traditional sphere of church, hearing the good news of Jesus for the first time.

I had always thought of France as being a Christian country - which it is historically and culturally, but the reality of allegiance to Christ on the ground is a different matter. It depended on who you asked, but most Evangelical pastors felt that less than 0.6% of the country was genuinely Christian. Even Catholic priests considered France a mission field due to the rising secular spirit and the growth of Islam, Buddhism and occult practices. It is said that there are more fortune tellers and faith healers in France than doctors - and there are lots of doctors in France!

As well as singing in the streets of Avignon, we also gave out tracts door to door. The title of the tract was *'Indifference'*, and, as I walked long kilometres from house to house, braving the high fences, barking dogs, suspicious stares and angry attitudes, I was beginning to learn something of the spiritual climate of France. It was encouraging getting to know the French folk. Gilbert Sanchez, was one of the first to receive Jesus through the outreaches and he introduced us to his family. His mum, Mme Sanchez, became an almost legendary figure and, after a visit to her home for a meal, you really knew why the French were famous for their cuisine.

"Mange! Mange!" she would cry in her well-worn 'midi' accent.

Coquilles St Jacques and 'flan' were her specialities, and it was almost a mortal sin not to finish the whole bowl she had prepared. I remember one particular day when she had cooked snails. Usually, in a French restaurant, if you order snails you would get a very hot dish with several round china thimble-like cups, each containing a ball of gristly meat soaked in parsley and garlic butter. It is quite edible and unchallenging. However, Mme Sanchez' snails really looked like snails! She would catch them in a cage, leave them to starve for a couple of days and then boil them up, shells and all, in a saucepan of water, adding some tomato sauce.

"These are my son's favourite," she said, emptying out a dozen very dead looking snails on to my plate, and giving me a long pin to pull them out of their shells.

"You can eat the intestines as well," she continued, while I contemplated the horns of the first snail on my plate. He didn't look that different from the ones I had seen that morning on the lawn.

"Come on! Eat up," she continued.

"My son ate a hundred last week!"

France is also a very beautiful country. It has everything from sea, lakes, mountains, gorges and green meadows. It is an enormous country marked by regional differences. General de Gaulle probably summed up France's diversity best when he said,

"How can you govern a country that has over 365 different cheeses!"

French individuality is, at one and the same time, its strength and greatest weakness.

Our teams enjoyed making the most of the beaches and rivers in the South and the Ardèche region. I never quite knew whether to laugh, cry or simply shrug my shoulders whenever we, as a group of Evangelical Christians - suitably clothed in unrevealing swimwear, would arrive on a beach to find we were greatly overdressed compared to the other less Evangelical bathers. I well remember one time when a group of more mature single ladies paddled out in a boat. In the middle of the lake, they unfortunately lost their paddle and splashed around in circles for a while. Imagine their relief when a burly young man swam up and began to tow them back to the safety of the bank. However, as he emerged from the water, their relief changed to shocked horror when they suddenly realised he was as nude as Adam!

The evangelistic teams also focused on Eastern France, in the beautiful Savoie region, where we would work with a Baptist Church in Chambéry. We spent many hours singing, doing drama and sharing the Gospel at the Place des Elephants and many people heard about Jesus in a meaningful way - a handful coming right through to becoming regular members of the church. We would stay in a beautiful chalet in the mountains, which had its own swimming pool and magnificent views. It was owned by a Frenchman of Russian descent called Paul Harbine who was a brilliant musician. He had rejected God in his youth after a friend had died of cancer. One day, whilst building his swimming pool, a piece of metal broke off the digger and hit him across the throat, severing the veins. Blood spurted out and he was rushed to hospital. While on the operating table, he actually died and had a vision of Jesus who sent him back to life - a new life of service and consecration to Him. He miraculously survived, committed his life fully to God, and built up the centre to be used by Christians. It really was a beautiful location and had a certain feel about it, as if indeed it was a special place, set apart for the Lord. It was in the Chambery Baptist Church that I preached in public for the very first time.

After that first Summer outreach, on returning to Llanelli, I was convinced that the Lord was confirming his call for me to go to France. I couldn't wait to get back. Confirmation of the call came when, after months with no regular monthly support, I was promised £60 per month from various supporters. This was the basic minimum I would need to pay my part of the rent for a council flat in Sorgues.

A month later, Peter - who was also working in France with the team, and myself hit the road to go back to Sorgues and set up a more full-time ministry of our mission, whilst working with the church. Our goal was to find a base for the work as the flat was unsuitable and, as the team would inevitably grow, we needed a boys' and girls' house. I was feeling rising excitement at the prospect of launching out on my first missionary journey.

As cash was short, we scrambled a lift with folks going to Paris and were then left to find our own way from Paris to Sorgues. After spending the night sleeping out in a public park, we awoke early and quickly got to the roadside to thumb a lift down South. However much we smiled or prayed, no one seemed to want to stop! After a few hours, we were getting fed up.

"What shall we do?" asked Peter.

"Why not get a coffee?," I replied, reminding him that he would have to pay!

Whilst we were sitting in the café, quietly minding our own business, an older man, who was totally out of his head drunk, came over and made the following offer.

"Bonjour! I'll take you anywhere you want to go in France. There is just one problem, I cannot remember where I have parked my car!"

We then followed him out to the car park where we walked around, looking for the missing car. After two fruitless laps of the parking, we were beginning to wonder whether it was all just a joke. Then he shouted out,

"Ah là voilà! - There it is!"

He ran over to a battered old vehicle that had seen better days. I didn't know whether to be glad or not. Feelings of trepidation increased as I watched him trying vainly to put his key in the door lock.

"He can't even see straight to get the key in the lock," I thought.

"How on earth is he going to manage to drive?"

Trepidation became fear as he finally opened the door.

"In you get," he said, and before weighing up the wisdom of such action, we responded.

My friend Peter, acting out of a stronger spirit of self-preservation than me, got into the back seat where, belted up, he braced himself behind his rucksack, preparing himself for the eventuality of any sudden impact. I, naively, took my place in the front next to our rather less than sober chauffeur. I comforted myself with the thought that perhaps he would sober up as the journey went on. I thought back to fiery sermons I had listened to about the missionary journeys of St Paul. He'd known shipwrecks, stoning and whipping, but drunken Frenchmen never appeared. So here I was, on my own missionary journey. What would happen indeed?

We pulled out from the parking, managing to dent and scrape a good number of the more affluent cars that had the unfortunate fate of being parked next to ours. I was encouraged by the more or less straight line that our intrepid driver was able to keep, but less encouraged when he wound the window down and began to shout obscenities to the various lady passers-by on the pavement.

"I'm not with him," I thought, reddening by the minute.

"I'm a missionary! I've come to bring the Good News."

The journey continued without too much difficulty and, as the man began to slur his words less, I wondered whether he might even find his senses again. However, before I could get too encouraged, he reached underneath his seat and pulled out another bottle of cheap *'Château Plonk'* which he proceeded to open with his teeth - cheap plastic top, before gulping down energetic mouthfuls.

"I wonder if I am doing the right thing?" I began to ask myself.

His spirit becoming more excitable, he leaned over to me and said,

"Would you mind holding the steering wheel for me while I put my sunglasses on?"

Like a twit, I complied, leaning over and grabbing the wheel while he continued to drive and delve into his pockets. As he placed the glasses on his nose, he said,

"Now, I'm going to see how much of a man you are," and he began to accelerate faster and faster.

Can you imagine it! Here I am, a young pioneer on his first missionary journey to France, full of vision for the future, and yet sitting vulnerably next to a crazed Frenchman holding the wheel of a car hurtling along at 90 mph! All sorts of things flashed through my mind as he accelerated.

"To live is Christ, to die is gain," quoted St Paul, but it didn't inspire me too much at that moment!

Somehow though, in spite of the immense foolishness of the whole thing, I felt sure it would be okay. The pervading sense of destiny and purpose seemed to overrule even the madness and dreadful insecurity of the moment. We were coming to a very sharp bend in the road and he was still accelerating.

"Oh no!" I cried, closing my eyes and jerking the steering wheel round.

I was expecting to turn over, spin wildly out of control and enter into oblivion. However, something strange happened. A miracle happened. Without even a forward jolting movement, defying all the laws of physics, we simply stopped dead. A sense of great peace filled the air, and there was our driver in a sleepy, trance-like state. Gently, we put him on the back seat and continued to make our way South to Avignon. Many years later, I recounted this experience to my friend, Peter, and asked him if he really did think it was a miracle.

"Yes, indeed," he replied.

"I think we were pioneering a new work in France and that the devil wanted to destroy it by sending the drunk driver. However, God intervened and saved us by miraculously stopping the car."

For myself, I'm sure that my own stupidity had at least as big a part to play in the whole affair as the devil's, but, without doubt, I know that God sent his angel to protect us on that journey.

Sometimes, when I get discouraged about my work, I think back to the fragile beginnings. Compared to holding the wheel of an out of control car, everything seems like progress!

6 'Les Griffons' and 'Rue des Dahlias'

We eventually arrived in Avignon. In the end, we developed a friendly relationship with the man in the car. It turned out that he lived in his car and was happy to travel all over France. Elijah, it tells us in the Bible, was fed by ravens, and God had certainly chosen this particular raven to get us back to Avignon and Sorgues to find the team base.

Our first port of call was to set up home again in *Les Griffons*, the council flat, or *'Habitation à loyer modéré'* – HLM, as they are known in French. When they were first built, these enormous megaliths of concrete were meant to be the ideal home for the rising well-to-do. However, most folks found the harsh anonymity of concrete and promiscuous contact with the neighbours too much to bear and moved out, leaving the blocks to become ghettos for the poor and disenfranchised – a magnet for the despised immigrant Arabs. Most of them came from Algeria, and a few from Morocco. Their ubiquitous families filled the dark, bulb less corridors. I first began to realise how much the Algerian war had wounded France when I met Alain and Patricia. Alain, himself the son of an immigrant, was in his early forties and should have been in his prime, enjoying life with his wife. Instead, he was an empty, broken man, full of anxiety, sleeping night after night with a loaded gun under his pillow.

As a young man, he had been conscripted into the horrors of the Algerian war. He had been witness to the barbarity of torture on both sides and his mind never recovered. Something snapped within and he spent the rest of his time, after the war, in a drugged daze, taking pills to ease the pain and erase the memories. He was a staunch supporter of the National Front, an extreme right wing group, which wanted to expel all foreigners from France, and whose policies and virulent attacks meant that the wounds between Algeria and France were even harder to heal. In spite of the hurts, they were a wonderful couple who delighted in pampering us single 'Brits' with the wonders of French cuisine. At the other end of the spectrum, were the young 'beurres' ('butters') - a self-assumed slang name for the French 2nd generation Algerians, whose 'bronzed' appearance, like the colour of butter, set them apart from the so called 'true' Frenchmen. They roamed aimlessly around the flats. Most of them were unemployed and just passing time with the ever-prevalent temptations of falling into crime and drugs. They were always very friendly to us, recognising in our own foreignness, a common bond. We lived in *bâtiment* HI on the top floor, which gave us plenty of exercise as there was no lift.

A local estate agent put us in contact with a small, furnished villa which was up for rent in the town. As we looked around, it seemed the ideal place to base the girls' flat and develop the offices of our mission in France. The rent was very reasonable, so we took another step of faith and signed the contract. It was very run down, but also very attractive with a nice garden. It had its own fig tree and a beautiful vine, which gave delicious grapes and covered the large front porch. It came complete with its own resident magpie who we called Fred. As we would worship the Lord in the front room, he would often come and join in, tapping the window with his beak.

A young Swiss lady named Sylviane, who had been called to work with our mission during our very first French expedition to North Africa, joined Claire and they set up home in the villa. It was house number 8 in the very quaintly named Dahlia Street. The girls were the Dahlias and the boys the Griffins!

Sylviane taught us to speak French and made sure we really spoke it amongst ourselves during the day. She also made wonderful soup on Saturdays which gave me and Pete a good reason to drop by on weekends to see if a light bulb needed changing! We put together a multimedia - drama, song and slides, presentation about World Evangelisation and began to visit different churches to promote the work of our mission and the call to serve Jesus.

I don't know how the French survived our atrocious English accents and numerous grammatical faults, as we presented the needs of unreached French speaking people groups around the world.

I began to work quite a lot with Sylviane in putting together our literature - she was a tri-lingual secretary by training, and, one Christmas, we were printing it all out on an old *Gestetner* press. I was getting quite flustered and annoyed as the printer wouldn't work. In a noble attempt to help, Sylviane tried to move the stencil, accidentally tearing it. I exploded and, from the overflow of my heart, spoke out a flurry of unmentionable swear words. I don't think she'd met a Christian quite like me before! At least she got to know me in a no frills way and, in spite of my rough and ready ways, we began to get along well. I had learnt French in the pubs of Paimpol in Brittany, so I'd picked up a lot of slang words. Often, after I'd preached in a church, she would gently let me know what rude words I shouldn't have used!

We had planned a promotion tour for Paris and Switzerland - to visit Sylviane's church and other contacts, so we were very excited to be on the road together. We had borrowed a large red Ford Transit diesel van from Great Britain. It wasn't the easiest vehicle to park in the back streets of Paris! We didn't have many church contacts at that time so we tried to arrange our meetings by directly telephoning various pastors from a public call box, asking if we could speak to their church. A good number refused, but we did manage to get a meeting at one of the largest churches in Paris. The meeting coincided with the battery on the transit going dead, so imagine our joy when the 1.000 FF we received from the church meeting exactly covered the costs of a new battery!

Paris is a beautiful city. It was also springtime, and Paris in the springtime is famed for its romantic atmosphere. That atmosphere must have started to rub off on me, as I began to look at Sylviane with greater interest.

After Paris, we headed for Switzerland. It was a first visit and, even though many people had said how beautiful the country was, I really was bowled over by the fairy tale beauty of some of the lakes and snow-capped mountains. We were able to stay with Sylviane's family who, at that time, were part of a Christian guesthouse, conference centre and old people's home called Bethel, situated in the Jura Mountains.

On one of our days off, we were able to go out walking in the snowy hills. Feeling like an adolescent again, I got into a snowball fight with Sylviane and we ended up rolling down a hill together, finishing up in a tangle of arms and legs at the bottom.

During one of our morning meetings, someone was sharing the story of Abraham and Isaac, emphasising how Isaac had to be willing to go up onto the altar in self-sacrifice. I felt personally challenged to greater consecration, giving up the final trappings of my old life. However, as I read on, I found that Isaac got off the altar and proceeded to get married. I felt the Lord saying that if I were willing to give myself fully to him he would take control of my life and that I would soon be getting married! I was flabbergasted. I could hardly believe that the Lord had spoken so directly to me through His word. I resolved to say nothing and let events work themselves out in their own time. So many questions were popping inside my head as we headed back to France.

"Would Sylviane be the person I was meant to marry? Did she even like me?"

After a couple of days back, I needed to do something.

"Oh Lord," I prayed that morning.

"Please give me an opportunity to speak to Sylviane today."

That lunchtime, Sylviane asked if anyone wanted to come with her to visit a lady who was sick in Avignon hospital. The opportunity was there, so I volunteered, adding an invitation to come for a meal with me afterwards. The decisive moment had arrived. Having got through the formalities of the afternoon visit, we now sat facing one another in a small café in Avignon's famed Pope's palace square. We ordered steak and chips and, while the meal was being prepared, I knew I had to say something. Tongue-tied, I began.

"Er, well Sylviane, how are you?"

I really didn't want to embarrass her and wondered how she would react to a declaration of love.

"This morning, I was reading in one of the Psalms that God wants to give us good things, and, well, I think that you are one of the good things that God would give to me. Sylviane, would you consider going out with me?"

There it was. I'd said it! And now for the moment of truth. How was she going to react?

Her face reddened, and then she replied.

"I've been waiting nearly a year for you to say that. Yes, I'd like to go out with you."

Wow! We were both so moved - so gripped by a sense of destiny, that when the food came, we were no longer hungry! We just sat there staring at each other! I picked at a few chips, but it was no good. I had another hunger now. We quickly paid for the uneaten meal and walked into the romance of the Avignon night. Isaac had found his Rebecca!

The rest of the team were delighted with the news, as were our respective parents. We were just going out, but I knew that things were serious. During a trip to England, my Mum gave me her old engagement ring, suggesting I might be able to use it.

A few weeks went by, and I invited Sylviane to dinner again. This time it was at the Pope's second palace - Château Neuf du Pape, a quaint village, famous for its wine. We went to a small restaurant called *'La Mère Germaine'*. This time I'd learnt my lesson. Before saying anything, I got on with the meal! After the meal, we went outside for a walk. It was a clear, star filled evening. A full moon shone, while the crickets gave their own natural rhythm to the symphony of the night air. We walked into a little olive grove and I got Sylviane to sit down on a rock. Then, in time honoured tradition, I got down on bended knee, took out the ring and asked Sylviane to marry me. She said *"Oui!"* and managed to get the ring on - even though it was a bit tight and I needed to get it enlarged later!

Before getting married - the date had been set for early November in Chambéry, we had to get through a busy Summer, running several evangelistic campaigns.

The British Ford Transit needed to return to Wales, so we faced the challenge of needing a new bus. This was our first real faith challenge as a small French team - an ideal opportunity to put into practice the principles of praying for finance which we had been learning. We decided that we would fast over every lunchtime, using the time to pray for a bus, putting whatever money we saved from the meal into the project.

The days became weeks, and the weeks months! As our bodies grew thinner, our faith grew stronger and money began to come in for the bus. On one particular day, we were led to pray specifically for £400 to come in. That morning, £100 was in the letterbox. In the afternoon, Sylviane had a surprise visit from a couple from Switzerland who wanted to support the work and left £200. Around 9 o'clock that evening, another £100 had anonymously - and mysteriously, appeared in the letterbox.

Looking back, we spent hours and hours in prayer for relatively little amounts of money, but it was this apprenticeship of faith which laid the foundation for the multiplied thousands of pounds that were to come in for the future work. Just before our July deadline, when the teams would be arriving, we finally had enough money and we joyfully broke our fast. We were able to buy a second-hand, white Ford Transit van, which gave faithful service to the team for many years, before it finally died in a slight road accident in the Ardèche.

The scene was set for another season of Summer outreach. A passion to share Jesus with ordinary French folk outside of the traditional church setting had always gripped us. We would often organise kids clubs in the council flats or do open air work in the streets.

One time, we were out with a group from Cambridge University who were particularly gifted musicians. One guy was playing the saxophone in the midst of a block of flats when a young couple came to the window waving at us with much excitement. The night before, they had been wondering about the meaning of life and thinking about God.

"If you really exist God," they had said. *"We want you to show us by giving us a sign tomorrow."*

They were overwhelmed when the answer came blasting in via a Christian saxophone under their window the next day! They became regular members of the small church in Sorgues.

The Summer festival in Avignon also offered many opportunities for effective, joyful street outreach. Music, mime, theatre, clown work and testimonies fitted in with the other street performers. We'd be out most afternoons with teams of thirty to forty folk, mingling with the thousands of tourists and local folks who would come for the Festival. Many of the students who joined us for these Summer outreaches received the call of God on their lives and are now serving the Lord in many different ways around the world.

The August trip took newly engaged Sylviane and myself to Apt in the Luberon valley where, with a French team, we were going to do some evangelistic work with a local French church. We were to be based in an old church. The only problem was that there was no running water, no loos and no beds! Just a big, empty hall! The time was a battle from beginning to end.

I remember one afternoon, when we had been preparing our drama sketches and songs in preparation for going into the town. On arriving in the town centre, there was hardly anyone there! Not to be discouraged, I proposed that we sing in front of the town hall as a proclamation to the heavenly realms that Jesus is Lord. As we began to sing, it began to rain! Still not wanting to give up, I persevered on finding an undercover location where we could still sing. Just as we began to sing,

"Avec les cris de joie – With cries of joy,"

a smelly dustcart pulled up right in front of us, leaving the engine running, while the driver went for a drink. It was all too much! The girl playing the guitar ran off in tears and I really did wonder if it was worth it. That night, after a particularly difficult time with the team, Sylviane came to me saying that if Christian work was going to be like this, she didn't think that we should get married as it was too hard to bear.

The next morning, the sun was shining, we had news of a contact during the previous days who had become a Christian, and the team was working well.

Over lunch, Sylviane said,

"I'm not sure if I meant what I said last night."

"That's alright," I replied.

"I wasn't listening anyway!"

Following the Summer, we busily launched into all the administration necessary in France to get married.

It was doubly complicated with us being British and Swiss. As the Church and State are separated in France, the legal marriage takes place in the Town Hall – La Mairie, with the blessing following at church if the couple so desire.

Although we lived in Sorgues, in the southern Vaucluse region, we decided that it would be better to be married at the church in Chambéry - Savoie region, where we had good friends and which also gave good access for Sylviane's family from Switzerland.

Our major challenge was to find a suitable venue for the marriage in Chambéry, which fitted the weekend of the 10/11 November. In the run up to this date, we had only one weekend free to get to Chambéry and find a place. We drove around, asking God to lead us to the best location, and we found ourselves led to a big supermarket on the outskirts of Chambéry, just off the motorway. There in the window was a big sign:

'Salle de noces à louer' - 'Wedding reception room for hire!'

We went in, enquired, and, just by chance, the man responsible for the room happened to be passing through at that very moment. We explained who we were, what we did and how we were asking God to lead us to the best place for a wedding reception. The man was quite moved by our testimony and, in just a short time, he had organised the whole thing for us. Room, meal, wine, wedding cake, the lot - all at a very reasonable cost.

The big day drew near. We decided that we would go for the civil marriage in Sorgues on the 7th November and then head up to Chambéry for the church wedding on the 10th. We saw the 10th as being our real wedding day before God.

Friends in Chambéry helped us with the organisation, and with the decoration of the church. At that time, I was a bit of a scrooge concerning money, and my faith in God's generosity was not yet mature. Sylviane wanted to buy some flowers for the church and reception. I grudgingly agreed, stipulating that she was not allowed to spend more than £10! She bought a few choice blooms and then trekked off to the meadows of the

Savoie to supplement the florist's meagre offering with the beautiful, wild flowers which were freely growing in abundance!

We had also been asking God previously for a wedding dress.

Sylviane has a good memory concerning that. We were visiting my Mum and Dad in Great Britain, when my Mum mentioned to Sylviane that she knew a lady who made wedding dresses. She invited Sylviane to come and just have a look. As they were looking, Sylviane felt that God was going to answer her prayer, especially as one particular dress had caught her eye.

"If this is the time to buy," she said.

"Give me a sign Lord."

My mum then said that she felt she should buy the dress for Sylviane and proceeded to tell the lady dressmaker that her daughter-in-law had been praying for the right dress and that now they had found it. The lady looked up surprised and began to weep.

"You know," she said,

"I really needed to sell a dress tonight and I prayed to God that you would be the answer."

God had wonderfully answered two prayers that night.

A further episode with the dress - or a bit of it, happened when Sylviane was getting ready for the wedding. She had gone to the hairdresser's that morning and had the veil plaited into her new hairstyle. One problem - she still needed to take a shower! I've often tried to imagine the scene of Sylviane in the bath with her sister holding back the veil, aiming the shower appropriately!

The wedding went well, with my twin brother preaching magnificently at the ceremony, and we had a marvellous evening celebration with Paul Harbine -the French/Russian who built the Chambéry centre, and family who brilliantly animated the evening with their singing.

A honeymoon in the mountains of Montana in Switzerland crowned a wonderful two weeks for us.

If the heart of history and Christianity is the love story of Christ for his Bride - the Church, then surely heaven and eternity must be even better than snow-covered peaks, romance, rest and passion! You can keep your harps and clouds, I'm looking forward to a celestial honeymoon!

7 A Growing Team and Family

A marriage made in heaven still has to live in the realities of an all too real earth with its conflicts and pains.

We began our married life sharing a team house and, despite the obvious inconveniences, community living helped us break some of the selfishness that Western married life can create. Although it is important for couples to have their own space and intimacy, it is also important to leave space for others. If the marriage monopolises all the time and energies, it reduces the potential for making friends and disciples of others.

Another early marriage memory was spending a month touring Britain in an Iveco van with two other folks, promoting the work of our mission via a multi-media presentation. It was Sylviane's introduction to fish and chips, English humour and endless cups of tea from our various hosts around the country.

Our team in France increased rapidly and we needed to find more accommodation. We were also asked to take on leadership of this growing team. So much for the tradition of not having much responsibility in your first year of marriage!

One morning, I was reading through my Bible when a verse from 2 Kings 4 v 16 seemed to speak deeply to me:

"About this time next year, you will hold a son in your arms."

I knew inwardly that the Lord was speaking about our first child and I was able to believe and lay hold of this promise.

Needless to say, the next September, Sylviane gave birth to our son, David, in Avignon hospital. I held him in my arms and praised God! In fact, I was so excited that on my way home I got lost!

A first child is an amazing challenge and experience. As young parents, you have everything to learn. It's incredible that God entrusted his only Son to the care of a young couple. The salvation of mankind hung on such a slender thread. Yet, by the grace of God, Joseph and Mary coped - and so did we.

Although no one knows the Heavenly Father except by revelation, every father gets his own personal revelation of parenthood via his children. David taught me so much.

One night, I was laying in bed, the gentle arms of Morpheus having cradled me into a place of tranquillity, when suddenly my personal nirvana was shattered by a strident scream and raucous crying!

"Waahh! Waahh!"

Thinking I was being attacked by some demonic banshee, I quickly awoke, only to realise that the baby was crying! Being slightly less than the ideal husband, I quickly nudged my wife in the ribs, waking her up and saying,

"Hey! The baby's crying. You'd better go and get him!"

And my wife, being the epitome of virtue, replied,

"It's your turn!"

She turned over to regain the comfort of pillow and blanket.

I crawled out of bed. The clock seemed to gloat as its luminous hands shone out 2.00 am. I had a headache and felt awful. I walked, zombie-like, towards the bedroom from where the crying was growing in intensity.

"Waahh! Waahh!"

The crying was building to a crescendo. I gingerly unpeeled the sides of the nappy and pulled it back. My worst fears were confirmed. My sense of smell went into overdrive and the huge mass of pooh which confronted me seemed to go beyond the realms of nature. How could so much come out of one so small? My headache was getting worse, every nerve of my body was crying out for sleep, and, as the wailing grew, I said out loud,

"Ah! Who'd be a father!"

I wasn't expecting an answer, but suddenly the atmosphere became electric as the Lord broke into my heart, speaking clearly to my inner man. In spite of the crying, a secret place of stillness opened within me, and I distinctly discerned the following words, echoing down from the heart of eternity.

"I'd be a Father. I was willing to leave heaven, become a man and save you from the mess of sin you were in."

I was deeply touched by this revelation. I realised that, so often, I was covered in the mess of sin, crying out to my heavenly Father. How grateful I was for his care and concern.

I quickly gathered the smelly nappy up and threw it away into the bin. I didn't spend hours poring over every detail of its content, but simply got rid of it!

Why do we spend so much time analysing our sins rather than simply getting rid of them at the foot of the cross?

I then got some cotton wool and that super white baby-cleaner liquid and, in the words of the famous boxer Henry Cooper, 'splashed it all over!'

The baby stopped crying, obviously feeling better at being clean. I couldn't help but think of the verses in the Bible which speak of being cleansed by the blood of Jesus. That historically shed blood is now applied, as a cleansing balm, by faith and repentance. Why stink when you can be clean? I put a fresh nappy on the baby and picked him up, holding him tightly in a warm and intimate embrace. He started to gurgle a smile and our eyes met in a covenant of love.

"Ah! It's not so bad being a father after all," I thought.

And the Father's voice, blown on the wings of the Holy Spirit, seemed to come again, bringing words of encouragement.

"You see, even your sin and repentance gives me an opportunity for deeper fellowship and communion with you. If you, a mere man, can love your own son in this way, how much more will I - your Father in heaven, love you and seek after your heart."

8 A Move to the Ardèche

We had a young and enthusiastic team, full of faith and hope for France and the nations. After each Summer outreach, a few would be called by the Lord to join us. The numbers in the team were quickly outgrowing the two flats and villa we had acquired in Sorgues. We began to seek the Lord for further direction.

One day, we found an unexpected letter in the post. It was from Sylviane's old boss in The European Mission Association - TEMA. He had heard about an old house that had been left to *La Mission Biblique en Côte d'Ivoire – The Ivory Coast Mission.* The house was very run down and being renovated by the Mission to be used as a guesthouse for their retired missionaries. It was situated in the town of Bourg St Andéol in the beautiful Ardèche region - famous for its gorges which attract thousands of would-be canoeists.

"As you have an interest in outward-bound work, I wondered whether you might be able to use this house in the Summer months," he wrote.

As I read those words, there was an inner conviction that this was important. Unfortunately, we then lost the letter and had to search frantically until we at last found it again! We were then able to ring the house in the Ardèche and arrange a rendezvous to discuss the possibility of using it as an activities base for the Summer.

We arrived at the house after long delays in traffic jams due to bad weather and road accidents. It was nestled at the angle of a dark and narrow street, named after the Protestant, Olivier de Serres. The entrance was in very bad repair, but we were welcomed by a delightful French couple into the comfortable apartment they had renovated.

As we sat talking, they explained a little about the house. It was what the French call a *'hôtel particulier'* – *a private mansion*, and was built by the De Bonot family in the 16th Century to celebrate their daughter's marriage. A very ornate iron balustrade and a sculpted plaster chimney were actually classed officially as 'historic monuments' which complicated the renovation procedure.

They explained how the Mission Biblique had inherited the property from a widow named Mme Magendie. It was a tragic tale. The Magendie family had acquired the building and lived there under the German occupation during the 2nd World War. Many memorial plaques around the town bear witness to the number of French men killed by the Gestapo during this time. For some reason, M Magendie was wanted by the Gestapo - some say it was because he was Jewish. They eventually caught him, beat him and finally executed him by removing his head. The savagery of this experience had a devastating effect on Mme Magendie and brought her to depression and eccentricity for the rest of her days. Like some modern day Mrs Haversham from Dickens *'Great Expectations'*, she hid herself away as a recluse while the old house fell into decay and ruin around her. The stray cats found a refuge in the house and the thick walls seemed to soak up the sadness of a lonely lady's life ruined by tragedy.

In her last days, she was visited by a friendly Protestant pastor. She asked him if he knew of a mission to whom she could leave her home. It was this pastor who mentioned the Ivory Coast Mission which, at the time, was directed by the famous evangelical statesman, Jacques Blocher. It was his vision to renovate the house under the name of *'La Fondation Magendie'* and use it as a rest home for retired missionaries. Unfortunately, after a good beginning, the money had run out for the renovation work and many questions were being asked as to the future of the vision.

On hearing his story, my mind went back to my own studies on the Rhone Valley area - and more specifically, to the origins of the town, Bourg St Andéol. It seems that this area had been very much on God's heart, and that the Holy Spirit had led the early church to target this region.

Jesus had stood atop a mountain in Galilee and, full of faith and authority, had given his rag tag disciples the vision and the mission to *"make disciples of all nations."* One of the more famous of these disciples was the apostle John who began to train a number of men, most notably Polycarp, who became Bishop of Smyrne in Turkey - today's Izmir. Polycarp, in his turn, made disciples of a number of men, including a young man named Andéol. Andéol, along with several others, was sent out on pioneer missionary work into the pagan land of the Rhone Valley.

The church historian, Eusebius, speaks of the 'Martyrs of Lyons', especially of the young slave girl, Blandine, killed in the arenas of Lyons and the miraculous healings, testimony and courage of the early Christians. Something very violent and very evil resisted the gospel in this area. Andéol travelled the Ardèche - then known as the Vivarais, with the same message of hope and salvation in Christ. He too, met with a violent end when a Roman legion - like the Gestapo of a future age, beheaded him. From the time of John the Baptist, whose head was set before Salome on a platter, it seems that the prophetic voice and Christian presence have brought forth much opposition.

A statue to Andéol in the Catholic Church of the town shows him with a sword through his head. Andéol's tomb can still be seen in this same church which became a place of pilgrimage for many. As I sat listening to the various histories of the house, I wondered if we too might find ourselves taking up the pilgrims' baton to plug into our own prophetic role in the divine strategy for France.

Later visits around Bourg St Andéol also brought some startling revelations. A major archaeological find - one of the few sites in Europe, was the discovery of a gigantic wall sculpture to the God, Mithra. Sandwiched between two natural springs - known places for pagan sacrifices, stands a huge mural depicting the sun god, Mithra, astride a bull. This pagan, Persian deity made major inroads into Europe and its presence confirmed the strategic nature of the town as a kind of spiritual crossroads.

The town was also home to a magnificent Catholic lady named Marie Rivier who opened up many Christian schools and was known to have said,

"If I can't preach Christ, I'd sooner die!"

A huge Catholic convent now does honour to her memory. Numerous statues, depicting a so-called Mary, crown the high places around Bourg St

Andéol, challenged only by other statues in honour of Diana, goddess of the moon and the hunt.

It was in the midst of all this that a house, in much need of repair, stood. The young couple invited us for lunch and they explained how they would have liked to see an evangelical church established in the town. They had begun a few tentative meetings in the house. As we ate, I became aware of my need to go to the loo, so I quickly got up and found my way to the toilet. As I stood there, finding relief, God clearly spoke into my spirit.

"You will go to the toilet here often!"

I'm not sure if my theology, or view of God, allowed Him to make such a dramatic statement in such a context. Having considered the lofty heights of sainthood, Persian deities and prophetic persecution, it seemed rather too mundane to receive my own prophetic direction in the loo! However, there was no mistaking the authoritative heavenly tone which my inner ear picked up.

"You will go here often! You will go here often!" seemed to have been planted deep within me.

I returned to my seat and we looked at possibilities for using the house in the Summer. We then took our leave. On the way back in the car, I shared with Sylviane what I felt the Lord had said to me.

"Do you think the Lord would have us live in that house?" I said.

"We'll see," came the wise reply.

Over the following months, we had several meetings with the directors of the Ivory Coast Mission to discuss possible involvement and partnership. We were in our own 'pioneer' stage and had no resources available to put into the house. They were unable to carry on financing the restoration of the building which became empty except for a local live-in caretaker. The house was hit by ferocious hailstorms and the lack of renovation and emptiness gave it quite an inhospitable atmosphere as time went on.

Over a year and a half went by and I had given up on my move to the Ardèche. The Ivory Coast Mission was willing for us to use the house, but we could not find a way of putting this into practice long term.

We needed to find a venue for a regional mission leaders meeting and I asked the Ivory Coast Mission if we could use the house. They agreed. We spent over two weeks in the house, caught up in much discussion and prayer, which seemed to give us a faith and boldness to take possession of 'our inheritance'.

At the end of the conference, I felt a number of our team should stay on in the house and start getting it ready as a base. In the meantime, I began to move all our team property from the flats and villa to Bourg St Andéol. I also gave in our notice on the villa and apartments in Les Griffons.

From this place of faith, and with 90% of our possessions already installed in the house, I phoned up the mission and explained to them my conviction that we should use the house and how we had already begun to move in!

"Are you happy with this arrangement?" I asked.

"Yes, okay," came the answer.

Nothing signed. No official papers, but we now had the use of our own centre! It amazes me to see how our progress in France has often hung on such slender threads. I sometimes wonder what I would have done if the mission had said, *"Non,"* rather than, *"Oui."*

Within three weeks, we had over fifteen folk working full-time in our mission family. A number of these folk went on to pioneer works in unreached countries of North and West Africa. Folk were sleeping in every nook and cranny that the house had to offer. It was decided that the renovated flat, which had belonged to the couple we first visited, should be used by myself, Sylviane and our little boy, David. And yes, I did use the toilet there often! In fact, the flat became our home for the next five years while we strengthened the growth and development of our mission base. The 'prophetic pee', as I irreverently remembered it, had indeed tied us into God's purposes for France and many other nations.

With regard to other nations, I had an interesting encounter as we were leaving our villa in Sorgues. Everything had been packed and we were having a last meal of bread and cheese in the garden, under the shade of our fig tree. Suddenly, a car pulled up with Mr Claude Moser, the then director of the Porte Ouverte mission, accompanied by a brother from the Central African Republic, Nicholas Ngarrasso. This brother was President of a very large group - *La Co-opération Evangélique*, of over 500 churches. We were still celebrating the birth of our first son, David, and our African brother was pleased to announce the birth of his daughter. We were able to give him a big white fluffy toy dog for her. He then proceeded to pray for us and bless us with a booming, enthusiastic African voice, full of power and authority. And so, a Central African blessing sent us forth to our new home in the Ardèche. Little did I know, how significant that chance meeting would prove to be!

We ran our first Summer outreach from the centre which became packed with over 40 students from British Universities. Apart from language and culture sessions, they would spend their evenings out on evangelistic efforts in the local flats of Bourg. The empty building was suddenly full of life - Jesus' life! I think this must have been quite a shock for the local inhabitants who must have wondered what had hit them!

When we moved into the house, we inherited a resident caretaker. He was a strange, friendly character. He seemed to have an unending supply of visits from all sorts of hippie types who were either in the town or passing through. I could not help but admire his zeal in receiving such folk so regularly.

My wife likes to look after gardens and, like most green spaces in the South of France, you need to be very faithful with the watering of plants. She noticed a whole crop of quite exotic-looking specimens growing in the back garden, but wilting under the heat. She made it her duty to faithfully water them at sundown each evening, and they began to thrive.

I came back early from the evangelism one evening and decided that I would investigate more closely these exotic plants as they had some familiar shaped leaves that I had seen printed on T-shirts in my student days. I inspected dozens of these growing, robust plants, struggling to recall what was written on those student T-shirts. Were they environmentalists defending some rare species? Did the leaves have some medicinal qualities? Then it hit me! The words, 'Legalise Cannabis' floated into my mind - my memory bringing back the proclamation that was framed in the famous green-leafed T-shirts!

"*Oh no!*" I sighed.

"*Our friendly, ministry to the hippies, caretaker is growing his own marijuana!*"

I lit a few dry leaves which had fallen from the main plants and was immediately greeted with the telltale smell of cannabis. I'm sure the mission strategy of such a conservative board as the Ivory Coast Mission did not include the winning of hippies via free cannabis distribution! The Jamaican singer, Bob Marley, had championed the Rastafarian faith, where members get high on cannabis as a form of worship. I was not yet ready - and trust I never will be, to trade in the Holy Spirit for cannabis.

I quickly sought out the caretaker and challenged him concerning his plants.

"*Oh, it's quite alright,*" he said.

"*Everyone in France is allowed to grow cannabis in their garden. You don't understand because you are English.*"

"*Okay,*" I replied.

"*Let's sort out this cultural difference by getting a short explanation from the local police.*"

"*Well,*" he responded, less sure this time.

"*I may be mistaken.*"

He certainly was mistaken! He allowed us to get rid of all the plants – we burnt them, trying not to inhale too much!

There then followed a long struggle, as our missionary community and the caretaker's lifestyle didn't always match. He was a nice guy at heart, but in the end, our roads separated and he ended up living in a mobile home in the next village.

We established an understanding with the Ivory Coast Mission that we would continue to renovate the house in exchange for a free rent. They agreed and we set to work. Scraping, building, plastering, painting – the years - or sentence, of centre management had begun!

God called a wonderful guy to work with us at this time. He was the world's best handyman and had a real gift of helps. He worked wonders on the centre with a shoestring budget. He eventually married a Canadian girl in the team who had a heart for the unreached villages of the Ardèche. In fact, marriage seemed to be the major ministry of the centre as many of the pioneer singles of our mission met their life partners.

The early monastic orders set up a principle called *'laborare orare'* – *'work is worship'*. This principle formed the basis of our team life together as we worked on renovating the house while maintaining much prayer for the nations and worship.

Our outreach was soon bearing fruit in the town and we began a small Bible study group with our contacts. In spite of the opposition and trials, which hit every pioneer work, we managed to start a small church.

One of our first converts was a former medium and fortune-teller. After a life in the darkness, occult and rejection, she was set free by the love of Christ and found light and happiness. We were able to baptise her in an open-air service in the town centre.

As the years passed, the church - wonderfully pioneered by a Franco American couple, needed to find its own local identity and outgrew the mission. It now has its own building and is pastored by a wonderful man from Mauritius. I remember discipling him in his early days with our mission and telling him,

"This town deserves a church."

This word touched his heart and, after his formal and on-the-job training, he was able to take on the leadership. He reminded me of this story when I was preaching in the church recently.

We were seeing spiritual fruit, but my own natural fruit was increasing, and our second son, Marc, was born in Pierrelatte hospital on the other side of the Rhone River.

The early days also included a visit to our team in America. I had the fleshly idea that I would be able to raise finance for our ministry there, but ended up coming home poorer than when I arrived!

Despite the local breakthroughs, my heart was still beating for the nations. Psalm 2 v 8 says,

"Ask of me, and I will make the nations your inheritance."

I was still asking!

Bourg St Andéol became a launch pad for a number of key ministries into the French-speaking world.

9 Tents, Tuaregs and Tea

The house in Bourg had been the incubator for several ministries into French speaking Africa, notably Niger and Burkina Faso. Pioneer teams were beginning in both of these nations with the goal of reaching out to the unreached peoples who included the nomadic Tuareg and Fulani tribes.

I felt strongly that I should recruit a small team of French people who could go to these two countries to pray and support the ongoing outreach. We managed to get together a team of seven folks - including myself, and we began to meet to prepare the journey. Cheap flights from Paris to Ouagadougou were booked on the infamous 'Le Point' airline - no longer in existence, and visas obtained from the Burkina Faso Embassy. We were aiming to get our Niger visas on the ground in Africa.

The big day came and we crowded into a packed plane. Hours later, we looked down at Ouagadougou - the capital of Burkina Faso, airport. The artificial environment of air-conditioned cabins was brutally shattered as we stepped out onto the blisteringly hot African runways to make our way through Customs. Bags and cases were unceremoniously loaded off the plane and strewn in a heap to be grabbed by their owners. Porters jostled and almost came to blows for the lucrative possibility of carrying a case or two while hundreds of hands, ranging from those of genuine beggars to opportunistic children, rained in like hungry birds hoping to catch a crumb of charity from the new arrivals - hot, aggressive bedlam!

Bags were opened and slowly searched while visas were scrutinised with excessive care. The minutes became hours before everyone finally squeezed out into the animated car park to be greeted by a chorus of eager taxi drivers and another battalion of hungry hands.

As it was my first ever trip to black Africa, I was feeling a bit lost and looking to find refuge in the form of our red-headed, white-faced pioneer from Cornwall. He had pioneered the setting up of two outreach bases in West Africa - Burkina Faso and Niger, two years previously. I looked as hard as I could, but the faces around me were distinctly dark and the crinkled black hair light years away from the fiery Celtic locks.

"There's no-one here to meet us!" I thought.

I had no plan B, and no idea of where to go in Ouagadougou. The others in the team were exchanging nervous glances, as they were also coming to realise that we were on our own.

We made our way to a patch of scrub, made ourselves comfortable and, in spite of the bustling bodies around us, began to pray and ask God to lead us.

Within half an hour, a red Peugeot pickup rolled up with an equally red headed driver. We all piled in the back and made our way towards a Bible School in the town of Koudougou, situated on the outskirts of the city. Darkness set in and we made our journey amidst a chorus of night noises, ranging from the croaking of frogs to the shrill cries of numerous animals. The excitement and energy of discovery and adventure mingled with the exhaustion of our bodies as we found a floor at the Bible School, unravelled our sleeping bags and sank into the sweet oblivion of sleep - a first night under African skies.

Awaking early the next day, Africa invaded our senses and captivated our hearts - colours, smiles, smells, abundant overwhelming nature, enthusiasm, strength and dignity.

The Bible School was run by the Assemblies of God church which was experiencing much dynamic growth in the south of the country. They had partnered with our mission team to launch 'Project Javelin' which involved two army trucks, filled with African evangelists and the *'Jesus Film,'* travelling to the unreached villages in the north of the country.

On arrival, they would contact the village chief and elders, asking permission to show the film at night, and run an evangelistic outreach throughout the day.

Permission granted, the team would then set up the projection equipment, screening the film onto the side of a lorry, using a generator for power. The whole village would turn out for the film and testimonies, followed by prayer for the sick. The African evangelists on the project were also in training and willing to serve as pastors for any new churches started.

After a first run of the project, it was estimated that over a thousand from different religious and animistic backgrounds had accepted the Lord. Several new churches had been planted as a fruit of this pioneer work.

We benefited from the good reputation the team had established and were very warmly welcomed. A wonderful man called Philippe Ouadrago and his wife, Josephine, showed us around the complex as well as giving us some valuable insights and teaching on African life and culture. We also heard about the work that was going on, learnt something of the African church and their vision for the future. Their heart was to reach out further to the Tuareg and Fulani tribes. We spent much time humbly praying with them.

Sunday morning was a fantastic experience as we split into three groups to attend the different church services.

Much is said concerning the poverty of Africa, but little is said about its richness. Seeing thousands of smartly dressed folks, Bible in hand, thronging enthusiastically to church to offer worship to God, is a deep challenge to our Western decadence. Little children, the holy light of innocence reflected on their faces, lift their hands in praise or dance enthusiastically to the worshipful drumbeats. Hours pass in worship and word and yet boredom and disinterest is not to be seen in this precious young generation - the true hope for Africa.

The shallowness of the instant satisfaction - via screen or sound bite, offered by the rich, materialistic nations, pales in comparison to the deep contentment and Godly glow which rests on Africa's vulnerability. We have everything in the West – yet lack the essential.

I felt embarrassed to be asked to speak in church, feeling I was very much the learner, but gave in under pressure and preached my first clumsy sermon in Africa. Little could I guess how the future would open up thousands more such opportunities.

As the days passed, our hearts became knitted to this land-locked country in French speaking Africa. Today, we have multi-national teams in several parts of the land, notably in Gorom-Gorom and Markoye, where the prayer for the Tuareg and Fulani, has been more than answered by courageous pioneers who have chosen to work amongst these peoples. Some of our folk, who totally identified with the local inhabitants in language, life and culture, have translated the scriptures into the Tuareg's Tamachek tongue.

I praise God for the small part our prayers had in laying a foundation for this ongoing ministry.

The time came for us to travel on to Niamey, the capital of Niger. This involved a long journey in the faithful Peugeot pickup. Our Cornish friend had pioneered the work in unreached Niger. He had courageously launched out on his own, and his first team was himself and two others. They had practically nothing to start with and they told me how, unlike most missionaries who arrive with some sort of vehicle to transport stuff, they had walked the dusty streets of Niamey, under the heat, carrying furniture , beds and mattresses as they set up the first team house. We were grateful for the recent acquisition of the Peugeot truck which facilitated our travels as we headed for the team house in Niamey.

Border crossings are never easy in Africa, and the border between Burkina Faso and Niger - on the road from Ouagadougou to Niamey, was no exception. We arrived mid-afternoon, but ended up camping overnight under the stars as the paper work and visa issues took longer than expected. Armed soldiers patrolled both sides of the border.

The next morning, we finally managed to cross and found ourselves at the Niger border just as the flag raising ceremony was going on. Flag raising is an important issue in many African nations, proud of their identity and independence from past colonial powers. We needed to stop our vehicle and stand to dutiful attention while the national colours of Niger were lifted up to the sky.

Unfortunately, one guy in our team had the habit of keeping his hands in his pockets and the soldiers saw this as an affront to their flag. Several of them shouted crossly and raised their rifles with menace in the direction of my absent minded friend. He was lost in his own world and didn't realise that the soldiers were shouting at him. He began to look around for what could be causing the problem, his hands still faithfully locked into his pockets. The soldiers thought he was disobeying them on purpose and became more and more agitated, with one even gently squeezing the trigger of his gun.

"Get your hands out of your pockets!" We desperately shouted over to him.

He finally understood, and went pale as he saw the rifles raised in his direction. His hands rapidly left his pockets and he put on his politest and most respectful look as he saluted the flag. The soldiers made sure he spent a long time standing in respect and we managed to apologise and convince them that it had simply been a misunderstanding. They let us travel on and we were pleased to leave the volatile situation behind us, wondering how many deaths and skirmishes in Africa might have had their roots in simple misunderstandings. It would surely be a shame to die for simply having your hands in your pockets!

The journey was breathtakingly beautiful and we followed some of the Niger river, watching fisherman in their dugout canoes gracefully reeling in succulent fresh water fish. We were grateful to arrive at the team house where we settled in and began to pray for the land of Niger and the next phase of our journey.

We got involved in some low key outreach and visiting in Niamey itself. A number of nomadic Tuareg people had brought their tents to the outskirts and shanty towns of the city where they had set up camp. It was the annual festival of *'Tabaski'* which involved the killing of a lamb. We were invited to an evening celebration.

A magnificent Tuareg man, dressed in his turban and richly dyed cloaks, warmly took me by the hand and walked with me. My Western culture was deeply embarrassed by the hand holding - quite normal in this nomadic setting, and it was just one of the many cultural lessons I needed to learn. The Tuareg men sang their traditional songs and danced. A number of them spoke French, so we were able to share with them how we also honoured the killing of a lamb - the Lamb of God, Jesus Christ. He was indeed a greater Son of Abraham than Isaac or Ishmael. He alone had shed his blood on the cross as a redemptive sacrifice for the sin of mankind.

We were also invited into their tents to share in the drinking of their strong, green tea. Each habitual gesture was measured elegance, as sugar and leaves were poured into a decorated tea-pot. Hot water, boiled over a charcoal fire, was then poured over it all. The pot was then skilfully lifted high and the sweet tea poured artistically into several glasses. It is said that this tea gives the Tuareg the endurance needed to live in the deserts

The Tuareg are traditionally closed to the Gospel, and only a handful have come to know Jesus as their Saviour. We were particularly fortunate to have a young Tuareg man on the team with us. He was linked to the mission team and was quietly developing his faith. It was encouraging to hear his testimony and listen to his prayers in his Tamachek language.

We felt that it would be good to travel up to Agadez to pray and support a French mission work which had been established there. The team had created strong links with this group ever since breaking down in their vicinity while on a mission trip which crossed the Sahara.

The journey was long and dusty as we travelled on the desert roads, meeting a variety of characters and scenery. We had our share of punctures and engine problems in the heat but, thanks to a gifted French mechanic who was on our team, managed to keep the vehicle going.

Agadez greeted us with its sights and sounds. One of its more famous 'sights' is an ancient mud-built mosque, supported with traditional wooden beams. Its 'sounds' range from the many tongues of nomadic peoples - who meet at this strategic desert crossroads, to the braying of donkeys as they pull their carts through the bustle of busy streets.

The French mission base welcomed us with traditional French flair and good food!

This work had been pioneered by a dear friend called Claude Moser. He told me how he had built up the base from practically nothing, risking life, limb and family to see a school and church established. He shared how the local snake-charmers of the town had sent their poisonous snakes after him one market day. Instead of giving into fear at seeing theses hideous reptiles sliding in his direction, he commanded them to stop in the name of Jesus. They turned around in an instant, ending up chasing the snake-charmers themselves who had to flee!

We were able to share in the local church and get involved in visiting various folks in the town. An English lady on the team had been building links with a nomadic, Tuareg clan in this area and she invited us to join her on a visit.

This was an amazing trip which led us into the heart of the bush and scrub. In the middle of nowhere, a wonderful, leather, Tuareg tent stood. The tents looked much more noble here in the desert, than those we had seen in the shanty towns which shamefully received those who migrated to the city.

The extended Tuareg family warmly welcomed us and pressed us to stay the night and eat with them. They specifically chose a young goat from their flock to slaughter later that evening. During the day, a few of us got together to put on a 'drama' to communicate the death and resurrection of Christ. We were able to perform this before the whole clan, many of whom responded very warmly. Others sang and gave their testimonies as well as they could with the limited translation skills available.

Later that night, the bleating goat was led away to have its throat slit. The blood soaked into the sand, and it was then skinned and boiled in a huge pot. For my Western eyes, used to seeing meat coming neatly packaged in plastic from a supermarket, it was all a bit too real! We then sat down to a wonderful meal together under the generous desert heaven.

As the night wore on, the Tuaregs silently slipped into the big tent, leaving us to sleep around the fire in our sleeping bags. However, there was a sudden thunderclap, clouds filled the night sky, and it began to pour down with torrential rain.

Everyone scrambled for the tent to find a place of refuge. It was a real squash, but a number of us were pleasantly surprised when we found an unused space, strangely free of bodies. I quickly unrolled my sleeping bag and stretched out under the shelter of the tent, enjoying my new-found territory. I couldn't help noticing, however, the smile on a number of the Tuareg men's faces. Later on, I realised why the space was free. I woke up with a goat weeing on me! Several other goats had installed themselves around me and I found that I was sleeping in the animal's quarter! My sleeping bag has never been the same since! The rain was still gushing down outside, but I was confronted with a more noxious liquid, drowning my romantic dreams of tent life with the Tuaregs!

The next day, we had the dubious privilege of living through a sand storm before finally making our way back to base at Agadez.

One of the French missionaries had pioneered a work amongst the Fulani and we were able to join him in one of his visits to a camp. The Fulani are nomadic cattle herders and we were able to spend two nights with them, listening to their traditional stories and sharing our own testimonies. Again, the nights were eventful times as poisonous scorpions regularly found their way into our shoes!

The work in Western Africa continues to flourish, and it is most encouraging to see indigenous workers, and a whole new generation of Brazilian missionaries, linking with the growing ministries amongst the Tuareg and Fulani. A major school, called *Anura – Light,* has been established in the capital city Niamey, which consistently provides a high level of education to hundreds of children from all backgrounds.

Our little French expedition came to an end, as we journeyed back to Ouagadougou airport, and boarded the plane homewards. We were encouraged to know that our prayers and contacts would continue on. Our eyes had been challenged by the visions of beauty that Africa had revealed, but also by the poverty and insecurity.

Our news media back home are often very quick to report on some new catastrophe or war hitting the continent. However, as we winged our way back to France, a proverb learned from the lips of a simple cattle herder - who drew on the wealth of Africa's collective wisdom, came back to my mind.

"L'arbre tombe à grands bruits,
Mais personne n'entend la forêt qui pousse.
The tree falls with a big crash,
But no one hears the forest that grows."

I silently prayed that the small seed we had sown might mature into future fruit, bringing blessing to these nations.

10 When the Desert Blooms

Having encountered God in a special way in North Africa, it was not surprising that this part of the world should figure as a major target area for our prayers and expeditions. Over the years, I was able to lead a number of French groups into these places. Memories of hot bustling souks, markets, generous welcomes, calls to prayer from the many minarets and endless quantities of targine and couscous come flooding back.

One particular group was very interested in the Southern Berber area around the city of Taroudant. A trip was organised. One member was a recently converted Reformed church pastor. We had been doing some Summer outreach linked with his church in the beautiful area of southern France called the *Vallon Pont D'Arc*. During this time - and challenged by the witness of so many young people, the minister realised that, in spite of his being a pastor, and in spite of his religious training, he didn't really know the Lord in a personal way. With great humility, he repented of his sins and asked the Lord into his life. He was subsequently filled with the Holy Spirit and became so on fire for the Lord that the Reformed church in Vallon didn't know what had hit it. They even raised a petition, trying to outlaw raised hands and clapping during the worship! My friend is still a Reformed pastor and, constantly growing in his love for Jesus, has become one of the church's leading experts on the Hebrew language.

Another member was an ex-prisoner who had been transformed by an encounter with Christ and now made his living selling baby's disposable nappies! We used his wonderful 4x4 Nissan Patrol to take us, in record speed, from the south of France to Tangiers. His wild driving brought back memories of another pastor – this time Pentecostal, who I had introduced to North Africa. He would drive at breakneck speed around blind corners, totally oblivious to the possible mortal danger of oncoming traffic! At one point, I made him stop and fled from out of his car, as his driving was too dangerous for me. I visited the coastal town of Tiznit with him where we were invited to spend the night with some friendly North African young men in their makeshift tent on the beach. We began to share about the Lord with them, when they started to light up some rather outsize looking cigarettes. As the pastor preached his Pentecostal heart out, the eyes of our friends glazed over and the tent was filled with a rather more pungent smell than incense! The preacher got redder and redder as the truth slowly dawned on him, and, when the local police decided to pay us a surprise visit, he saw the potential end to his promising ministry.

"Pentecostal preacher in drugs den!"

He could already imagine the headlines in the paper. However, no such headline ever appeared as the police were used to the nocturnal anarchy of the area and realised that we were there as naive, religious men.

The very next day, I found myself in Rabat, at the office of the Bishop of the land, trying to work out some partnership agreement on how we might work together. This time, the smell really was incense, and instead of a glazed response to the gospel, I was confronted with the polite political correctness such an office demands. I didn't feel tremendously satisfied with the trip, but the Lord has His own ways, and, amazingly, the Pentecostal Pastor is today leading the French Reformed church in Rabat, doing an excellent work for the Kingdom of God.

So our team arrived in the area of Agadir, en route for Taroudant. One afternoon, we drove out to a very wild piece of the Atlantic coast for a swim. Without thinking, I plunged into the sea, intoxicated by the powerful waves, enthusiastically jumping over them as the current led me deeper and deeper into the heart of the ocean. I looked back and was shocked to see how far out I was and began to worry when I saw how hard it was to swim against the current. I paddled hard for a moment trying to get back, but realised that I had made no real progress and had only held my own against the current. Worry grew to fear and fear to exhaustion as heavy waves crashed menacingly around me. I cried out to God and, in the midst of the noise and brine, felt an inner strength as fear gave way to faith.

With much effort, I managed to circumnavigate the current and made some progress back, but found myself being washed upon very jagged rocks. I then had no choice but to go with the flow as I was so worn out. The waves spun me over the rocks time and time again, but I finally emerged - bruised, bleeding and bedraggled, onto the awaiting sanctuary of the beach. My friends ran over to gather me up, tend my wounds and care for me. The local inhabitants had told them that most people who were washed out to sea like I had been, ended up drowning. In fact, someone had drowned there only the week before! I had benefited from a fortunate escape.

All these years later, I still bear the physical scars from that time on my legs and, when I look at them, I think that they are a parable of our lives and trials. We often fight against the current in worry and fear. The important thing is not to give up, but to find an inner strength, through faith in Christ, and push through the challenges. We may often find ourselves bruised and battered - but never defeated.

Arriving in Taroudant, we were greeted with the many faceted demands of hungry hands, smiling faces and clever merchants. The heavy spirit of an unyielding religion infused the atmosphere of the place with a fatalistic hopelessness. I had felt encouraged to search out any Christian allies by trying to find out if there was a Catholic presence. We were led to a big wooden door, wedged in between high, imposing walls. After some energetic knocking, a warm faced, grey haired man opened the door to us. Clear blue eyes, that seemed to find their light from some deep inner source of spirituality, silently greeted us and gave us the assurance of hospitality and welcome.

We were then led into the most magnificent of gardens. Literally hundreds of fruit trees were growing with their luscious crop of grapefruits, oranges and bananas. Ornamental fountains gushed generously from deeply dug wells, and myriad bright flowers danced in the fragrant breeze. The garden itself seemed to be elevated beyond simple earthly beauty to a vocation of worship to the Lord in this dry and dusty land.

This was the home of Père Christophe Leclerc - a Franciscan monk who had dedicated more than fifty years of his life to the service of the poor in North Africa. A simple chapel, surrounded by several out buildings, provided rest and refreshment for us.

Père Christophe was a man of prayer, and he generously shared his life with us while we stayed with him. During the war years in France, he had decided to help the Jewish people, but found himself arrested and sent off to prison camps in Germany. He was in the same prison as the famous Protestant theologian Dietrich Bonhoeffer who was later martyred. Bonhoeffer said that when Christ calls a man he calls him, *"come and die,"* and Père Christophe seemed to be one such living sacrifice for the Lord. He would never speak of his sufferings, but would simply look beyond to some distant place of communion and emphasise that God is love.

Père Christophe was from a large Breton family and he had another brother who had also taken up the priestly vocation – and who also shared in the horrors of Nazi deportation. He was known as a famous writer in France. *"La Sagesse du Pauvre,"* by Eloï Leclerc, was the story of Francis of Assisi. Two brothers, taking the vows of poverty and service in the name of Christ. How amazing it was then to learn that another of the brothers had decided to develop the family shop. The "shop" became *"Leclerc"* supermarkets which is now one of the biggest chains in France - something like the equivalent of *"Sainsbury's"* in England. This brother Leclerc was one of the most affluent men in France ! What contrasts of destiny.

Père Christophe asked us to sign the visitors book and, as I wrote my name, I could see that the previous visitor had been a certain Bernadette Chirac - the wife of a famous French President. Père Christophe, from his quiet place of prayer in this hidden garden in Taroudant, was obviously an influential man.

Over the years, we made several visits to this centre looking to partner together in the setting up of a prayer base for North Africa. On one visit with a Swiss group from our home church, I was accompanied by Sylviane and our two little boys, David and Marc. After a harrowing drive over the dangerous Tiz'n'test pass in the fog, we arrived at the tranquillity of the centre. In an unguarded moment, David made the most of his time by picking as many slightly less than ripe grapefruits as he could from the trees. We ended up with dozens of them. It takes maturity to recognise the time of ripeness.

We made lots of friends in Taroudant itself. I remember befriending a man who ran a small souvenir shop in the bazaar. He was from the Saharawi tribe where there are no known Christians. Over the days, confidence developed and I was able to give him a Bible in Arabic. A few months passed since the next visit, when I found he had been put in prison. I managed to get permission to visit him in the squalor of his overcrowded prison cell. He was a broken man, looking to be free from the passions which bound and shamed him. Other prisoners squashed in to hear as I shared a prayer of hope and left him with a seed of faith to go with his Bible.

Another young man joined us on our travels and again, over the days, became convinced of Christ's claims and gave his life, through a simple prayer, to the Lord. Sadly, I later learned that he had been harshly persecuted for his faith and had even had to spend time in prison until he renounced his beliefs. For such a young believer, the pressure was too much and we were unable to have a renewed contact with him. Another sad end awaited our projects for collaboration with the prayer centre vision. The powers that be preferred to let the centre go to a hotel developer who destroyed most of the garden to make rooms for tourists. Père Christophe retired to Aix en Provence in France where I was able to visit him from time to time. His eyes would sadden when he thought about all that had been given away in Taroudant, but an inner light of faith would shine forth from within – from a hidden recess of his soul, where the lessons learned through loss and suffering gave a living expression to the verse which says.

"Unless an ear of wheat falls to the ground and dies, it remains only a single seed . But if it dies, it produces many seeds."

This lesson was to be re-learned many times over the years as we developed ministry into North Africa. I found myself overseeing a pioneer work into the bustling, overcrowded town of Constantine. Looking back, I was not experienced enough to build on the sacrificial foundation of intercessory prayer that had been laid over several years, in preparation for the launching of a young couple into this challenging area. It was also a very difficult time for the nation itself, in the grip of civil war, religious fervour and frustrated democracy. This lead to much brutality and insecurity within the country, teetering on the brink of total anarchy.

Constantine was also a stronghold for traditional values and anti-Western attitudes. However, it was also a town of many smiling faces, hungry for affection and affirmation. We linked with a Congolese pastor who bravely ran the "Eglise Réformée" in spite of opposition and racism. People would cruelly insult him and his family and empty rubbish in front of their home. In spite of this, I can remember the place being packed full of eager young men as we shared the gospel through music and testimony. I remember climbing up the cliffs surrounding the town where a Roman monument to the "Winged Victory" dominated the city. As we looked down, we would sing out the Lord's reign - not through the conquering sword of the Emperor Constantine, after whom the place was named, but through the humble brokenness of a weak and vulnerable man on a cross.

Our missionary couple were also weak and vulnerable, lambs among wolves, yet filled with a dignified love for their neighbours that transcended the shame of failure, persecution and pain. A trusted contact ended up denouncing us and we found ourselves written up in the newspapers as a dangerous group. Fortunately, they put the wrong address and names on the article so little damage resulted. The persecution grew stronger against Western symbols, culminating in the brutal assassination of several French Franciscan monks. Love was stretched to breaking point and, under increasing pressure from home churches, the couple were pressured into pulling out, leaving the town - even to this day, with no evangelical witness. I remember being asked the very difficult and pertinent question of whether such a city was a "suitable place" for this particular couple. I could only reply with another question.

"Was the cross a "suitable place" for Jesus Christ?"

Seeds had been sown in North Africa, but, somewhere in my heart, I also felt a longing to sow seeds into the great continent of Asia as well.

11 A Letter from Cambodia

"I cannot tell you how wonderful it was to receive this gift of a beautiful book - the Bible in Khmer, which I had never seen, nor read before. I am reading it and re-reading it almost each week. It teaches so many things. I am trying as well to tell its story to my friends... Almost all of my friends, who are students of Khmer literature, ask me frequently if I would like to sell it or give it to them – they would like to have it at any price ; so I lend it out to them for a week each."

And a few weeks later :

"Dear Sir,

I want to tell you that all those who have read the book that you gave me have begun to believe in the person of Jesus Christ, and that the number of readers of this book is growing day by day and more than ninety have begun to read it since December 1990."

Tears filled my eyes and wonderful memories flooded my brain as I read these letters, which were the fruit of a journey to South East Asia in October 1990.

For a number of months before, I had been burdened about developing missionary links into Indo-China and I began to pray with another friend about this. In the "upper room" of our Bourg St Andéol centre, many hours were spent trying to overhear God's council concerning such a visit. The Lord gently revealed to us that we should take a prayer team into three cities – Bangkok in Thailand, Saigon - Ho Chi Minh City, in Vietnam, and Phnom Penh in Cambodia.

We recruited a prayer team of nine people and began to make all the necessary preparations for flights and visas. Things seemed to be going well until, after months of planning and preparation, I received a phone call from my key Asia contact saying that there was no way that they could get the necessary documents for entry into Vietnam and Cambodia! I had nurtured a secret dream of travelling overland from Ho Chi Minh city to Phnom Penh, but my dream seemed to die a death as I phoned folk up to tell them the news.

Praying over the situation, the Lord gave me Revelation 3:7-8

"I have placed before you an open door that no one can shut."

This verse seemed a bit ironic in the face of an only too real shut door! Sylviane, my wife, also received the passage about Jeremiah buying a field in a hopeless situation. With these verses in place, and with faith in our hearts, we decided to fly to Bangkok anyway and see how the Lord would lead us.

My wife was pregnant with our third child as I left for the trip. It was one of the few times that she cried on my leaving, as she was not sure if I would be back in time for the birth. I also shed tears on the long drive up to Paris airport.

We left on a Sunday afternoon with Air Tarom - Romanian Air, to Bangkok. Although Air Tarom was cheap, I cannot say it was very comfortable and the seats seemed to have been specially designed for inducing the maximum amount of suffering for the longer legged amongst us! We had the privilege of a three hour stop over at Bucharest which enabled us to pray for the country at a critical time in its history.

On the plane, I was able to share my faith with a leading Romanian politician who had spent 15 years in prison under the previous regime. He was head of the Christian Democratic Party, although he himself was only nominally Christian. I was able to give him a New Testament in Romanian that he was overjoyed to receive.

My feet trod Asian soil for the first time as we left the crowded plane and entered the even more crowded airport at Bangkok. Street vendors were selling myriad trinkets and exotic smells spoke of the equally tantalising morsels that were cooking on innumerable itinerant barbecues. Belching exhaust smoke, a strident symphony of car horns, chaotic traffic jams and beautiful, ageless smiles welcomed us to just another day in a crowded Asian mega city.

An American missionary guesthouse had been willing to reserve rooms for us, so, when we finally found our way through the culture and crowds - trying not to get too ripped off by the taxi drivers, we arrived and set up base in our comfortable rooms.

Shining Buddhist temples stood tall on most corners and, coupled with endless carved depictions of various winged monstrosities and other deities, seemed to give strength to the spirit and identity of the city. In trying to understand the powers behind such a spirit, I came to the conclusion that, apart from the obvious pagan, animistic idolatry - which can be found in many religions, the ultimate philosophy was to reach a state of passive "no desire." This passive spirit is in contrast to the Christian experience - which indeed dies to self, but rises in Christ to a passionate, pulsating new life.

If Buddhism is *"no desire,"* Christianity is *"pure desire."*

We began to pray together as a team and sensed that the Lord could still open doors into Cambodia and Vietnam, even though, in human terms, it looked impossible. The Lord seemed to be saying that our faith would open such a door.

After some wonderful river rides on the local "boat bus" and much searching, we found an agent in Bangkok who was able to set things in motion for visas and flights again. Our missionary friends had warned us against such agents as they often left their clients stranded in Vietnam, having overstayed their transit visa, and with no possibility of a return flight. In spite of this, we decided to take the risk and go for it.

The prospect of the door opening into Vietnam lit a fresh passion in our hearts and took us into deeper realms of faith and prayer. After our week in Bangkok, we found ourselves en route for Vietnam on a three day transit visa, with a promise of a possible visa for Cambodia in Saigon, and no confirmed return flight!

Arriving in Vietnam, we got through customs and stepped out into a world of bicycles. The young, the old, families and officials were all moving majestically in great waves of wheels, spokes and bells. I even saw a couple of pigs being transported on a very heavily laden cross bar.

Ho Chi Minh City is the victorious name given to replace the defeated decadence of old Saigon, with its memories of French colonialism and American GI's. Some of the past magic of Saigon still lingers in the decrepit architecture and seedy bars which fill the place. We were very much learners as we struggled to find our way around, but soon learnt that the dollar was still a mighty currency which crossed all language barriers and gave the lie to the communist utopia.

A friendly taxi driver took us to the Kim Do Hotel in the heart of the city where we were able to live like kings on the few dollars we possessed. The average wage in Vietnam at that time was a mere eight dollars per month, so our little money went a long way, including lavish meals in "homely" street restaurants for under a dollar. I'm not sure if we really were eating the rump steak promised in the menu and were more likely coming to grips with the spiced up remains of rat or dog!

We also concentrated on our prayer mission, asking that the "bamboo curtain" would fall as the Berlin wall had done. On our last night in Vietnam, we felt a real breakthrough in prayer and worship. Heavy, divisive spirits seemed to constantly resist the progress of prayer, and several in the team felt led to speak out against spirits of civil war and destruction.

Ho Chi Minh City is another Asian metropolis with millions of people living by their wits and the sweat of their brow. This, coupled with the decadent past of Saigon, has also given rise to a "bar girl" culture where drinkers are paired up with beautiful, obliging hostesses. We had promised our American hosts in Bangkok that we would deliver some Bibles to the local Christians, so I set off with another fellow to deliver our promised package of God's word. Imagine our surprise as, faithfully following the address indicated by our missionary friends, we found ourselves bang in the middle of one of these bars, surrounded by adoring young women! It turned out that the bar did in fact belong to some Christian leaders which gave rise to some interesting cultural interpretations. The Bibles were gratefully received and we felt pampered and refreshed by the beautiful, perfumed hospitality. Bible smuggling has forever taken on a new dimension in my experience! Honour intact, we left later that evening, amazed at the grace that incarnates in the most unusual of places.

One of the folks recruited for the trip was a young lady named Solange. Although she had been born in France, her parents had been refugees from

Vietnam, escaping the ravages of war and poverty. This was her first trip to the land of her ancestors, and she had a dream of meeting up with her long lost grandmother whom she had never known. She possessed a scribbled address which led us out into the countryside surrounding the city. We created quite a stir going into some of the villages as they were not used to seeing foreigners. A number of young ladies seemed to be quite interested in me and kept giggling and pointing in my direction. I felt flattered, so asked Solange - she spoke fluent Vietnamese, what they were saying. I was quickly deflated when she said they were saying how big my nose was! Asians have little noses.

It was especially moving to see Solange meeting up with her 80 year old grandmother who saw her long lost granddaughter for the very fist time. Tears flowed as they hugged one another tightly in an embrace that transcended the years of separation and suffering.

Warm hospitality once again greeted us, and we were privileged to get some genuine insight into Vietnamese family life. We were able to share our friendship and the truth of God's love in Christ as our chopsticks deftly shovelled in tasty morsels of rice to mouths open with the joys of fellowship. It was sad to say our goodbyes at the end of our time together.

On returning to the city, we spent a lot of time at the Cambodian Embassy trying to get our visas. The officials stressed how dangerous it was for us to visit the country at that time, with pockets of rebel soldiers still on the loose. Things got very difficult at one point which forced us into an impromptu prayer meeting in the consulate itself.

After an initial refusal, I sent the team off to buy food and remained in front of the Embassy, eating an orange on the front porch. Suddenly, a very irate Ambassador emerged, bustled me into his office and agreed to give us visas to travel by plane to Cambodia. I was amazed at this sudden turnaround. As he looked through the passports, I remembered our prayers back in France when I had specifically felt the Lord wanting us to travel overland between Vietnam and Cambodia as a sign of a new beginning for these nations.

"I'm, sorry," I mumbled

"Although I'm very grateful for your willingness to give us visas, I really must insist that we have the visas for overland travel."

The Ambassador exploded with rage and shoved me out of the Embassy again. Once more, I sat on the steps praying and peeling my second orange. To my astonishment, before I had finished my orange, the Ambassador appeared again and, pulling me back into his office, agreed to give us the visas for overland travel. What's more, he offered us use of the two Embassy cars and their drivers! Even today, I ask myself:

"Why the sudden change in the attitude of the Ambassador?"

I've no firm answer other than the miracle of prayer, but an experienced missionary to Asia once mentioned to me that if someone wants a favour, he humbles himself by either fasting, or eating little, at the doorstep of his master. I still wonder if my oranges had something to do with the miracle.

The highlight of our time was the overland journey into Cambodia. We had air conditioned Embassy cars and my seat was lined with the insignia V.I.P – a very important person indeed!

Earlier on in France, we had prayed to be God's Ambassadors in this country, and His answer was more than abundant. We got through customs with no hassle - even though we had overstayed our transit visa by 2 days. I'm sure the Embassy cars had something to do with that leniency.

As we crossed into Cambodia, to be greeted by luscious green rice fields, sugar palms - which stretched endlessly on the horizon, and heavy horned water buffalo, the driver put on a Khmer wedding song. It was sung by a famous Khmer singer who had been killed under the Pol Pot regime. Going past the flower filled pools which framed happy villages, streaming with young children, the music seemed to be singing out hope and resurrection for the land, proclaiming a prophetic message that Christ was coming in praise and glory to take up his Cambodian bride. The beauty and the presence of God were so real and powerful, moving many of us to tears. In that instant, the power of the prophetic celebration of Christ's victory was greater - and more substantial, than the demonic destruction of the killing fields of Pol Pot!

We arrived by night into the calm of Phnom Penh, which was still in a deep process of reconstruction. It was before the arrival of the U.N forces and the big business companies. Cars were a rarity and, like Vietnam, our dollars went a long way. We found our way to a quiet hotel where our drivers left us free to roam and explore. That night, as we prayed in the "Asia" hotel in the heart of Phnom Penh, our hearts were bursting with thankfulness to God.

I am the proud uncle of a young Cambodian man. My brother in law had spent a year working with the Quakers in Cambodia as a prosthetics specialist. During that time, he and his wife felt led to adopt a young Cambodian child. We visited the orphanage where they had found their son the year before. As we arrived, a nurse came up carrying a minuscule baby who had just been found dumped in the garden. Our hearts broke as we saw the crumpled body and wordless prayers rose silently, as we longed for the child's survival. The incident brought home to many of us the pain of a world where babies are dumped. Jesus is the only one able to bridge into this suffering world and bring healing.

"Please use us Lord, your Body on earth today, to bring a measure of healing to the nations."

We were well received and honoured wherever we went. We were also able to visit a hospital and a prosthetics workshop. We attended a Sunday night meeting for ex-pats and were able to encourage the often tired and overworked aid workers to find new refuge and strength in worship. Needy places and people need to be able draw on the supernatural life of Jesus, in order to see genuine transformation.

It was so amazing for me to see the openness of the population to the Gospel. I spent one Sunday afternoon sitting alone on the banks of the Mekong River. Person after person came to chat and practise their English or French. It was the first time in my life that I had spoken to so many people who had never even heard the name of Jesus, and who had absolutely zero knowledge of the Gospel. It was an immense privilege to simply witness and share the basic truths concerning Christ and His love with these young men and women. All were very open - not tied by Buddhism or atheistic doctrine to a very strong degree, and were hungry for Bibles. We were thrilled to have shared a deep and intimate contact with two young Cambodian students in particular. We were able to give them a couple of Bibles in Khmer which we had brought with us.

The letters at the beginning of this chapter are from them, proving how the seed of the Word has already produced much fruit.

I truly sensed an openness and imminent harvest for this much troubled land. Phnom Penh is a very beautiful capital, and a walk by the Royal Palace, on the banks of the Mekong, is a delight.

It was in Phnom Penh that I tasted snake soup for the first time in my life. It made it worse, seeing the live snakes in a cage at the entrance to the restaurant! Snake tastes very much like fish for those who are interested.

A grim reminder of the tragic past of Cambodia was given as we took a look around the Tuol Slang museum of genocide. 17000 people were killed, imprisoned and tortured in this converted school. It was gruesome looking around and seeing the tragic blood stains still on the floor, grisly reminders of the hidden horrors of anonymous suffering. Photos of the murdered men, women and children - their eyes full of fear and death, were pasted onto the walls which seemed to buckle inwardly, like some tired megalithic scrapbook, containing the pain of a lost generation.

It is said that the Pol Pot regime killed between one to two million folk in its insane transformation of a nation. One of the most poignant tragedies of all this was that the guards, who did most of the torture and killing, were often not more than 14 years of age. Some of these guards, at the time of our visit, would have been 24, fighting for the Khmer Rouge cause in the Cambodian jungle. Recent television documentaries - June 2003 in France, have interviewed these "school boy" torturers who are now grown men, living in a changed Cambodia, but trying to come to terms with the guilt of the past.

War was still very real for Cambodia at the time of our visit. On the day we drove back through torrential monsoon rains, we saw many heavily armed soldiers en route. At one crazy place where we had to take a ferry, a young soldier fired his gun just in front of our car. It brought folk running, and was all a bit tense for a moment, before calming down. The day we left Phnom Penh, there were gunshots and fighting in the city.

We prayed much for the healing of the nation and the strengthening of the

Church. We also asked for our own mission to be able to send out workers, with long term creative solutions, to bring blessing on the Cambodian people. The years have passed, but a powerful work is now thriving. Several teams are now involved in a multitude of ministries which are bringing hope, prayer, salvation and employment, in Christ's name, to many young men and women. *Care for Cambodia* – an N.G.O founded by dear friends who were inspired by our first trip, rescues trafficked youngsters who have been sold or abandoned to the sex trade, giving them a warm home and a hope for the future.

We had an eventful 12 hour journey back to Ho Chi Minh City. Driving through the night, on the busy roads of Vietnam, was a mini nightmare! We still had no places for our return flight, but felt confident the Lord would provide. We queued, argued and finally resorted to prayer, waiting hours at the ticket offices. After telling the vendors that we were "VIP's," sent by the highest authority, we finally got two places on Air France and three on Air Vietnam - the last person getting a seat, with only half an hour to spare, before the take off!

We unwound, reliving our dreams and adventures in Bankok for a day, before boarding our flight back to France. A friend picked me up at the airport and I spent some time with his family before leaving at 3 a.m. to drive the many miles back home to Bourg St Andéol - our base in the Ardèche. I arrived ten hours later for the end of our Sunday service. I was pleased to see Sylviane, who was, happily, still pregnant with our third child. I got back just in time for the birth.

A little baby girl called Déborah came into a world of hope and promise. Her prospects were very different from the majority of little children born in Cambodia. We prayed that she would become an *"eleventh hour worker"* for Christ among the nations.

Cambodia is still a nation seeking to move forward into all that the Lord has for it. Justice still needs to be done, and lives still need mending. However, we can rejoice in the many miles already travelled, and in the steady growth of the infant Church. I was recently at our mission conference in Spain where I renewed my contact with my friends from *"Care for Cambodia"* who have given themselves to love and rebuild this nation.

Their eyes shone as they told me of how the work had grown and been blessed. Bright eyes then filled with tears, as they were overwhelmed with the sheer beauty and grace of the Lord, who can bring so much healing to the hurt and broken places of the world. Love and celebration will surely triumph in the end.

May these ancient killing fields truly become living fields.

12 Touching Africa's Heart

In Chapter 8, I spoke about a chance encounter with a certain Nicholas Ngarasso, the then President of a large denomination in Central African Republic - a nation nestled in the heart of the African continent. We had given him a little white fluffy toy dog for his newly born baby girl.

The years passed, and we became aware that the future of missions lay less and less with the traditional sending nations of the West, and more and more with the emerging Christian nations of the developing world, who were experiencing much growth and revival.

The Lord was challenging us to become "mission planters" in such lands. A prayer developed in my heart for an invitation to French speaking Africa. One Summer, I found myself teaching at a camp near Chalon sur Saône where I was introduced to a missionary couple, Claude and Jeannine, who were linked with a group of churches in Central African Republic. We shared our vision of mobilising the African church for mission and they invited us to come and run a seminar for their churches.

The Welsh apostle, the founder of our mission, joined me on these early visits and was able to lay down a strong foundation of intercessory prayer. I well remember our first trip to Bangui, the capital city of Central African Republic. A power cut plunged the airport into total darkness and it was every man for himself as panic stricken hands grappled for various pieces of baggage. Running the gauntlet of rapacious custom's men was also a unique rite of passage into the beautiful, vibrant anarchy which is Central Africa.

The nation gained its independence from France in 1960 after having much of its previous population depleted through the ravages of slavery. The country rarely made the headlines except through the infamously unhappy reign of Bokassa - who ruined the nation's economy at his horrendously expensive coronation ceremony as Emperor, and who committed atrocities to keep his hold on power. He was known to have won the favours of the former French President, Giscard D'Estaing, by offering him diamonds, which are a much misused natural resource of this country.

It was a relief to see the smiling face of Claude awaiting my arrival. His faithful Land Rover gave valiant service over the potholed tracks which went by the name of roads. He loaded up my meagre baggage and took me straight to a meeting with the church leaders.

"We've just had a major tragedy," he confided.

"The President of our denomination has been killed in a road accident!"

He mentioned that we would be seeing the widow and the man's family at this meeting. We arrived at Lakouanga church which was the base for the 500 other churches in this massive African denomination. On arriving, I gave my regards to the widow, but found myself captivated by the well worn fluffy white dog being held in the innocent hands of his six year old daughter. It suddenly dawned on me that the man who had been killed was none other than the same man who had prayed all those years ago at our house in Sorgues. Beyond the obvious sadness, I felt a sense of destiny and a mandate to redeem something from this loss for the ultimate benefit of this nation.

Another small, unimposing man looked on and was introduced by Claude as being the new President of the church association. His name was Gabriel Gatfosse Yerima. A small man in physical stature, but a giant of a man in prayer.

He had been a pioneer in bringing revival and church planting to the unreached, Pygmy peoples who lived in the sprawling Equatorial Forest of Central Africa. He shared with me how he had walked hundreds of miles through the forests to bring the message of the gospel to the Pygmies. His words were accompanied by many miraculous signs and healings. On one particular journey, he found himself walking on an kind of mound only to discover that it was an enormous poisonous snake! The snake literally lifted him from the ground and sank its fangs into his leg. The deadly poison quickly touched his nervous system and he began running like a madman through the forest. Miraculously, he was found by a group of local Christians who spent three days nursing and praying for him. Just when everything seemed lost, Yerima received a vision of the risen Christ and found himself wonderfully healed. He was now responsible for many thousands of Christians in the country who affectionately called him "Baba" or "Papa" Yerima. He was indeed a father to many in the same way as Abraham was called to be a father to many nations. His prayers and welcome helped us to establish the work in Central African Republic.

He invited us to spend several days in the forest town of Scieplac which had grown out of his evangelistic efforts amongst the Pygmies. Two days driving on forest tracks, passing huge trunked trees and taking in the breathtaking beauty of waterfalls, myriad butterflies, birds and wildlife, brought us to the village of Scieplac. Tragically, whole areas of the forest were now devastated as greedy wood exporters, hungry for the ebony, acacia and other expensive woods, thought nothing of destroying hundreds of trees to gain access to the one they wanted to cut. Such ecological genocide was destroying the natural habitat of the Pygmy peoples and also that of many rare plants and species.

The Pygmies welcomed us with great joy and enthusiasm. They lived in little leaf igloo dwellings which adapted well to their nomadic lifestyle. They loved music and dance and it was an amazing experience to see them dancing rhythmically around the huge night fires. They have a particular polyphonic way of singing which transports the listener into an ethereal world of awe and wonder. One of their songs rang out,

"We bring nothing into this world, we will take nothing back," echoing a distant wisdom which could even find its interpretation in our Bibles of today.

Yerima encouraged us to pray for the many hundreds of Pygmy groups that were still scattered throughout the forest and who were still without any evangelistic witness. It was amongst these Pygmies that I first discovered the culinary joys of caterpillars and monkey!

On the journey back, we were presented with a tortoise which is the traditional meal to honour a tribal leader. I sat with this live tortoise, crushed up in the back of the Land Rover, for many hours and miles as we journeyed back to Bangui, the capital city. I grew quite fond of my shelled and scaly companion who grew more and more confident to pop his head out and survey the surroundings. Unfortunately, he popped his head out for the very last time in Bangui, was grabbed by strong African hands and plunged into a pot of boiling water! The next time I saw him - or part of him, was when a plate was set before me, containing a clawed and scaled foot, floating in a peanut sauce. As the honoured leader, I was obliged to take enthusiastic mouthfuls while my heart was rather less inclined to be scoffing my travelling partner. I mean, tortoises are family pets where I come from.

In Bangui, we were able to run a seminar entitled,

"Central African Republic – A light to the Nations."

In spite of many foreign mission agencies and thousands of full churches on the ground, the country was yet to see its own indigenous mission movement. Our goal was to find the key men and women who had already received the vision for mission in their hearts, and to encourage them to push forward with their dreams. We also felt that much local initiative had been ruined by the unwise handouts of money which only fuelled jealousy and dependency. Because of this, we resolved from the beginning, never to give money, but to offer our ministries, prayers, words, vision and fellowship - which ultimately required more sacrifice than a few easily given dollars. This was very much going against the grain of traditional Western mission in that land, and many groups, finding that we were not simply a push over for easy money, lost their initial enthusiasm. However, it also drew the quality people who had genuinely received a vision from God for their nation.

At the end of one tiring day, having been slightly disappointed by the number of folks who had chatted to us only in the hope of getting money, we were ready for bed. Another young man pushed forward, insisting on speaking to us. As he spoke to me in French, my Welsh companion said :

"Look, if this is just another fellow looking for money, tell him that we really are not interested."

The young man looked across at my friend and replied in good English.

"Let me assure you Sir, that I have not come for your money, but I have a vision from God on my heart."

We were suitably embarrassed by our suspicions and sat down as he unfolded his story. His name was Anatole Banga and, although growing up in a wild, animistic family, he had managed to fight his way through to education and study. He even managed to get a scholarship to study agriculture in China. Gifted at languages, he was able to learn Chinese and came into contact with the Chinese underground church. As he saw their tears, prayers and love for Christ, his own heart softened and he gave his life to the Lord. He then found himself discipled in this Chinese church and, in his turn, called to serve this movement amongst his fellow students. He also gained a scholarship for the Haggai Institute which trains up and coming third world leaders. At this institute, he had the opportunity to emigrate to America and begin a ministry there. This was a huge temptation for a young African man from humble origins, but - as he prayed, he felt the Lord asking him to go back to Central African Republic and set up an indigenous mission group that could send African missionaries to the unreached parts of the world. He had helped found a church called, *"La Fondation Jerusalem,"* and was keen to see how far we could work together. Anatole has since become the major player in building mission in Central African Republic.

Another man who crossed our path was Cyriaque Bomba Bengabo. He was an evangelist with a large church grouping called, *"Action Apostolique."* He had studied in East Germany and had returned to his country with strong political ambitions. These ambitions had seen him sent to prison - he was falsely suspected of a bombing, and he found himself only hours away from a firing squad. It was during this desperate time of incarceration that he began to pray and seek more than his Marxist dialectics. He found Christ - the way, the truth and the life. After training in a Bible school, he went into the unreached towns and villages to plant churches. He had no fixed income and so he developed creative ways to fund his ministry. First of all, his wife started making doughnuts which she would sell in the markets. He began making mud bricks which he was also able to sell. He trained some of his first converts in how to make the same kind of bricks and, before long, they had managed to build their own church as well as having quite a healthy business running. Cyriaque's heart was for self-help projects that could provide work and social development for his corrupt and poverty stricken nation. Cyriaque, Anatole and Pastor Yerima formed the nucleus of a missionary movement which was to bring hope and transformation to the entire nation.

As we prayed and worked together over the years, we came up with the name, *"Nations En Marche,"* as the title for this African missionary movement. There were three major thrusts to the work.

1) Missionary outreach to the most unreached people groups, both within and beyond the nation.
2) Intercessory prayer and fasting with the establishment of 24/7 houses of prayer for the nations.
3) Business As Mission. The teaching of business skills so that entrepreneurial gifting could be released for the setting up of self-help works that would not only defeat poverty but also finance the missionary thrust.

Anatole was able to set up a small *"Polytechnique"* training school, operating under these three principles. Students have been able to start pioneer works amongst the Pygmy and Fulani peoples of C.A.R. and others are now moving on to Chad and beyond as the work grows. Hundreds have come to the Lord, lives have been saved through the setting up of basic health care, children are learning the skills of reading, and the vision still burns strong for this holistic African gospel to spread further afield.

To understand the challenge of all this, you need to take into account that C.A.R. is one of the poorest countries in the world with the highest incidence of A.I.D.S. in Francophone Africa. It has known severe political violence, with at least 4 coups over the last years, and much fighting amongst the different ethnic groups. Only the prayers of the people of God have kept the country from falling into destruction, civil war and anarchy.

Over the years, we have been able to pray with several of the Presidents. On our very first trip - having barely arrived in the country, we were granted an audience with David Dacko, a former President, who was an inspirational source of information concerning the history of the nation. I was also asked to pray with General André Kolingba, who also had his stint as President, following a coup.

A few years ago, I was invited to eat and pray with another President - Ange-Félix Patassé, who was keen to mobilize the 'Nations en Marche' team to help transform his nation. Sadly, he died in mysterious circumstances in a hospital in Douala, Cameroon, before the context of collaboration could be created. One Central African lady in our team, who has a distinct ministry of intercession for her nation, was able to play a key role in bringing reconciliation to the political arena.

At present, Central Africa Republic has descended into chaos with the invasion of the radical Islamic group *Seleka,* and the counter attacks of the Christian militia, the *Anti Balaka.* The present leader of the nation – a lady called Mme Samba Panza is a good friend of my Central African colleague and has even been to pray with us at our base in the North of France. She needs much wisdom to know how to turn her country around.

Several years ago, during a visit to the Pygmies in the Equatorial forest, I was able to see God break into the life of the son of the most infamous President, Bokassa. This story, along with many others, is included in the next chapter. The following accounts are little snap shots of the live, on the ground action which has been taking place over the last few years – little cameos of God's grace and dealings with a nation.

May these true events give you hope and prayer for Africa which is so often portrayed as a hopeless case in our news media. A song from South Africa says :

"We see a new Africa."

And this is indeed my hope and prayer, as we push through the tragedy and the anarchy, into all that the future has to offer.

Tears For Souvenirs

A well known song begins, *"Tears for Souvenirs,"* and that could well be a description of one of my first visits during a military coup. While most of the missionaries were being evacuated out, I found myself on one of the last "Air France" flights going to Bangui. The folks on the ground were surprised to see me arrive amidst the armoured vehicles and myriad soldiers at the airport. Every day, I was emotionally out of my depth before the courage and dignity of my fellow African brothers and sisters.

Anatole's wife, Odile, had just seen armed soldiers shoot down the doors of her house, nearly killing two children who hid under the bed. As she fled with the family to the safety of another area, her husband left for a conference in South Africa. Her little girl, Ariel, went down with malaria.

As Odile struggled with thoughts about her lost home and the shock of the last weeks, tears welled in her eyes. I can still remember her crying and praying through the nights as I was sleeping in a neighbouring room. Yet such dignity! She insisted on cooking and cleaning up after us missionaries. She refused self pity, considering our own comfort and food more important than her own situation.

The same pained dignity shone in the face of Pastor Yerima. He had been in the bush when trouble broke out in Bangui. His van had broken down which left him a difficult two day journey - standing room only, back to Bangui through endless check points, manned by ruthless soldiers. Ethnic cleansing was already rearing its head as people who happened to be of a different tribe were dragged off the bus and shot by the soldiers.

Yerima used his spiritual authority and influence to protect a deacon he was travelling with who was from one of the persecuted tribal groups. His health had broken down due to the stress of everything. He had heard that his young cousins at University had been killed by vengeful militia, as well as hundreds of other such stories.

"You know, these ethnic problems are the fault of the church," he confided in me.

"We started the divisions within our own churches and it is now spreading to the nation."

Suddenly, overwhelmed by the burden of prayer he was carrying, he broke down weeping. All of us in the room felt the weight of the moment, as if God's own heart was weeping, and all we could do was humbly weep alongside.

My friend Cyriaque also had his own story to tell. He had been on the run for a week as various factions wanted to kill him. He had been instrumental in saving hundreds of lives as he had been able to give a warning concerning an impending bombing which annihilated a whole district one night. He was also living in the dangerous South side of Bangui at the time, where over a 100.000 people had been displaced because of the bombing and revenge killings of the various militias. He explained to me how his little girl had gone into shock during the bombing and was suffocating. He ran out into the night as the shells were falling, carrying his daughter in his arms.

"Will you pray for me Rob," he said, his eyes moistening with tears.

"Things have been hard."

I could go on - the Rwandan Tutsi pastor who had walked 3.000 km through dense forest with his Hutu flock to arrive at a refugee camp in Bangui, the young girls who broke down in church after nearly being raped by the soldiers. The list of such personal tragedies was endless. And yet, far from descending into despair, these folks carried a powerful dignity and strength which transfigured their suffering.

Revelation 7:13-17, speaks of those coming out of the tribulation. These folks have *"come out"* of a great tribulation. Tribulation and injustice are like unholy fumes which penetrate the atmosphere and impregnate the hearts of innocent victims of tragedy. This is why the holy ones needed to,

"Wash their robes and make them white in the blood of the Lamb."

Victims of tribulation need to be cleansed from the hurt by the blood of the Lamb, who suffers with them. However, the pain, once cleansed, leads them to the presence of God.

"They are before the throne of God and serve him day and night in his temple."

Serving God day and night in his temple - see Luke 2:37, is the life of intercession. In God's mysterious, sovereign purpose, He uses tribulation to prepare intercession.

I believe that the Lord has been building his altar in Central Africa through the tears and suffering. The French translation of Psalm 6:9-10 says:

"The Lord has heard the voice of my tears."

I believe He has heard the collective sorrow of this nation throughout the years, up to this present crisis, as it rises through tribulation to become an intercessory force for good. The *"Slain Lamb"* at the centre of the throne of God -Revelation 4:6, epitomises the dignity and beautiful mystery of a love that dares to weep and bleed. His wounds are real, eternal, and yet pure and beautified.

"No angel in the sky, can fully bear the sight,
But downward bares his burning eye
At mysteries so bright."

God cleanses and redeems our sufferings. As I was thinking of the 100.000 displaced peoples who were the innocent victims of this coup - lost children, the weak and aged, with no medicine, sleeping out in the bush in the middle of the rainy season, the rest of the Revelation passage seemed so real :

"He who sits on the throne will spread his tent over them."

The very best shepherd is the one who has learnt to be a lamb. God is gently shepherding this nation – and the many other millions of refugees in the world, to the living waters of His healing Presence.

"For the Lamb at the centre of the throne will be their shepherd; he will lead them to springs of living water. And God will wipe away every tear from their eyes."

Hallelujah! He is healing the land and the hearts and, gently, as a Father to his troubled son, wiping away the tears.

In the midst of the trials, we were able to continue with our mission building seminars which included a significant session at the Parliament buildings in front of 600 people, including the Home Office Minister. Many people came to the Lord. A highlight for me was an open air meeting in a very volatile area, preaching in the light of a full moon under African skies, to over 500 folk who had gathered.

However, the ultimate blessing was the last night when we finally managed to get together with all of the *"Nation en Marche"* leaders for a night of prayer. It's hard to explain, but the Lord was very powerfully present, and the five hours passed like five minutes.

Every prayer was pregnant with prophetic utterance and, while we prayed, I could see clearly that God was building his altar in the Land. It was a fulfilment of the word from 2 Samuel 24:18 that the Lord had given for the time:

"Go up and build an altar to the Lord on the threshing floor of Araunan the Jebusite."

Although the country was on the verge of civil war and destruction, I believe the Lord used the prayers of many in Britain, France and elsewhere to turn the country back. We had been in prayer and fasting for 3 days before leaving, and, from the same passage in Samuel, had found the faith to speak out against the angel of destruction:

"Enough! Withdraw your hand!"

From our arrival, the cease fire began, the mutiny ceased and normal life started again. A healing of hearts is always necessary, but God is patiently pursuing His purpose and the tree of life stands at the crossroads of history, bearing fruit each month and giving leaves for, *"the healing of the nations."* Revelation 22:2

African poet, Mongane Wally Serote, wrote :

"Blood, no matter how little of it, when it spills, spills on the brain, on the memory of a nation."

Irish poet, Seamus Heaney, sums up our hope for the healing of such blood tainted memory when writing in *"The Cure at Troy."*

"History says, Don't hope
On this side of the grave
But then, once in a lifetime
The longed-for tidal wave of justice
Can rise up
And hope and history rhyme.
So hope for a great sea change
On the far side of revenge
Believe that a further shore
Is reachable from here
Believe in miracles
And cures and healing wells."

I am still believing in the miracles and healing wells. Such wells and miracles are needed more than ever in Central Africa today. Adversity has never prevented us from pushing forward in mission, and it must count as one of my life's privileges to have been able to share in the daily routine of the Pygmy peoples.

I spent so many happy days with them in the magic of the Equatorial forest. My poetic energies and idealism ran wild as I watched the beautiful butterflies glide on the wind, and I danced with pure joy and abandon in the fire filled Pygmy celebrations. Let me share the poetry with you.

Pygmies, Prayers and 'Papillons'

Early man found himself in a beautiful garden with trees, fruit, streams and the perfect presence of God...Paradise.

Caught up in the heavenly songs of a hundred polyphonic Pygmy voices, a forest for our Cathedral, and dozens of multicoloured butterflies gliding on the wind of prayer, I heard an echo of that distant garden.

God gave an authority to early man to reign, and, in a realm way beyond human strategy and modern machinery, I discovered an authority amongst the early peoples of this Central African Republic. An authority of life in harmony with earth, but, as redemption works its purpose, an authority in prayer to usher in the chosen destiny of a nation.

It was the pursuit of this hidden destiny in the heart of Africa that led our brave brothers in C.A.R. to give their all to pioneer a work amongst the Pygmy clans of Bobelé.

The Chinese have an ideogram word for 'New Beginnings' - a buried seed with a long root beginning to sprout fresh green shoots above the ground. The pygmies also have a word for 'New Beginnings' or 'New Thing' : *To Yé'* – '*Tow-Yeah.*' It's the word they use to describe God calling creation into place. A new beginning. A new thing.

"See, I am doing a new thing !
Now it springs up; do you not perceive it."

God has worked a quiet miracle in the secret of the Equatorial forest. The African team which we were able to establish here have won over 100 of these unreached peoples to the Lord over the last years and have been involved in the delicate task of discipling them.

Total joy emanated from the evenings of worship, dancing in a circle around a huge fire, sending myriad sparks up into the star filled African nights and bringing memories of God as he appeared in a flame to the shepherd Moses, or as he spoke of a multiplied family to nomadic Abram as he contemplated his own African heaven.

It's hard to evaluate the worth of a little basket, woven with wise dexterity at the hands of a young Pygmy girl, and then carried with effortless grace on her head, or the greeting of a grey haired elder, honouring a visitor, his muscle bound frame and noble bare feet, speaking of years of dignified labour on the earth. Western clothes are not well adapted for the natural wear and tear of forest life, and, maintaining a minimum of dignity with the coverings the forest provides, the more hidden clans teach a long lost secret about lack of shame and self consciousness.

My many years of visits to this people, teaching the Bible and God's love, has to rate as one of life's deepest privileges - and challenges! I had to throw away every book and prop of Western thinking and theology. Who's teaching who I wondered?

Leaning heavily on the crutch of grace - every step being a prayer for help, I discovered that mime, theatre and song were the means of communication, rather than preaching words - albeit through a translator, at them. The best times were ones of group activity where everyone got a say in creating the word God was giving. I was absolutely amazed to see that they could compose a new song - usually the word in their dialect that the Lord was giving, within five to ten minutes, and then sing it joyfully together for the next 15 minutes.

We acted out their own creation mythologies before going on to make a mime and song of the Biblical creation story. My greatest joy came when I realised that they had grasped the secret of prayer as I listened to the joyful ode they had composed from John 14:14.

"You may ask me for anything in my name and I will do it."

I'm sure that part of Jesus' *"joy set before him"*- even through the sheer suffering of the cross, was to see the nations of the world owning his word in their cultures.

Pygmies rejoice the heart of Jesus!

New beginnings are also the fruit of suffering, and even the most hard hearted atheist would confess, along with the poem of Milton, that this world is now a *"Paradise Lost."* One can also hear the echo of sin and suffering within the now 'fallen' forest.

The "little brothers" shared how some of their oppressors - nearly every other African tribe, forced them to sell their blood cheaply so that they could then sell it on for profit to the hospitals! The grossly enlarged feet of elephantiasis, the swollen bellies of little children - the legacy of malaria, and horrendously infected wounds also testified to the curse of illness.

The missionary team pulled a little girl back from the brink of death, caring for her and sending her to hospital - at their own cost, in Bangui. She got well and blossomed under the care. I met her smile a number of times during my stay. Amongst her early problems had been syphilis in her blood. Shocking, and yet the reality of the demonic infestation of paradise. Healing and redemption had became real possibilities to her because of a few acts of selfless love. However, on her return to the clan, her family - not yet belonging to the Lord in the fullest, wanted her back in the old ways and exposed her once more to the destructive, animist traditions.

Over many patient years, at the request of the Pygmies, the team has struggled to put in place a sustainable health care project and a literacy programme. Several have begun to discover the joy of reading the Word of God. Creative, God inspired solutions have been prayed into existence.

During our forest gatherings, a number of different groups from other African tribes in Central African Republic come together. Africans love prayer and I was totally stretched to the limit when I discovered that the twenty four seven prayer meeting they had set up would only be interrupted by the teaching sessions!

Soaked in the atmosphere of prayer, I got used to the manifestation of dreams and prophetic utterance and action that came forth from our times together.

At one session, God seemed to be cleansing and healing the conscience of the nation as we prayed for three generations of leaders. The old, the now and the future *"Joshua"* generation that will rise in pure intercession to lead Africa into its destiny.

At another session, a prophetic mud brick was laid and anointed as a sign of a *"Joseph"* – a missionary movement, being birthed in the forest. Anatole Banga - the leader of Nations en Marche, had been praying about basing his training in the forest, and the brick may well be a sign of a 24 hour prayer house and "Centre for the Nations" being established here in the future. I couldn't think of a better place for pioneer missionaries from around the world to be trained.

We ended the teaching sessions with a night of prayer. At about 2am in the morning, an anointing came on the praying and I heard the 'sound' of nations on the march!

It is a new, non-western, energetic, vibrant, wild and powerful sound! It is the sound that lies in the hearts of this new African generation - and no doubt in the hearts of multiplied thousands from the new missionary armies around the world.

Each nation will bring its 'sound' to make up the redemptive harmony of a new world.

"To Yé Bobelé!"

13 The God of Pygmies and Presidents

The reality of Central African Republic and the Pygmy work has had an enormous impact on my life. When I think back to my Dad's prayer all those many years ago in the orphanage, could he ever have imagined that some of the answer to that prayer would end up in the Equatorial forest!

I've already described the joys of living with such a noble people, but I feel I cannot let you leave this wonderful forest without sharing another truly remarkable story.

I was invited to be part of the initial pioneer African team which made some of the first contacts with a certain Pygmy tribe. I had the privilege of cutting my way through the Equatorial forest with them as they began their missionary work.

We finally found a group of about 50 - from 5 clans, who gathered in a makeshift leaf church to hear the gospel. I was the first white man who had ever visited them. It was quite an event. Eager, innocent hands touched and pinched my white skin, while others ran their fingers through my hair, shyly laughing to one another. I felt ashamed as their simple, corporate gaze exposed the sophisticated veneer of my inherited Western culture of selfish individualism.

"How on earth do you minister to an unreached Pygmy group?" I thought.

In our weakness the Lord graciously led us to the Biblical passage in John 13, where Jesus – a humble servant, washes the feet of his disciples. In the same way, we were to wash the feet of the tribal leaders as a sign of our desire to serve this neglected people who are, unfortunately, despised in their own country.

I stood up and asked them to explain their own creation stories to us. They eagerly told us of a friendly, generous God who had made the forest and all the living creatures. Sadly, this God was now separated from them and they had to placate and honour a host of other little gods in order to survive. After listening and sharing some food with them, they invited me to speak. I stood up and, speaking in French with my friend Benjamin who translated into the local language, began.

"Would you like to know what your great God who made the forest is really like? Do you want to know His heart?"

"Yes," they replied, taking my words very seriously.

I grabbed a traditional wooden jar and filled it up at the nearby river. On returning, I got all the elders to sit down on a long branch before us. I gathered the missionary team around me and gave them each a cloth. Together, we got on our knees before the Pygmies and began to wash their feet.

Every eye was transfixed by this ritual which seemed to communicate more than mere words. My eyes filled with tears, that splashed into the bowl of water before me, as I held the well worn foot of a tribal elder - a foot which had never worn shoes and which had journeyed many long and faithful miles under the leafed canopy of the beloved forest. I'm sure that Christ's feet, covered in the dust of Galilee, must have looked more like those of the noble Pygmy, than my own pampered "plates of meat!"

The African missionaries' eyes wept too as they repented of the prejudice and crimes that their clans had committed against this indigenous people. They prayed inwardly that their future service and consecration would give flesh to the symbolic healing and cleansing that was being illustrated in this forest sacrament.

The Pygmies themselves seemed to have a profound respect and communal understanding of what was going on. A deeper revelation was at work in their collective intuition and wisdom.

"If God is like this, we would like to continue in His teaching," said some of the Pygmy leaders after witnessing such a moving event.

"We welcome your African missionaries to live with us and teach us more about God."

I went back to France with these words of welcome ringing in my ears and many questions as to how our vulnerable mission team might survive in the forest. Could a work which blessed the Pygmies – the poorest and most rejected people of the nation, end up transforming the whole country from the bottom up?

The next year at home was filled with much prayer concerning all of these issues, as I prepared for a follow up visit to the Pygmy clans. I'm so thankful to my colleagues who were willing to spend hours seeking God's face with me in all of this.

In the month leading up to the trip, I had the conviction that I should write up, in French, all the revelation God had given over the years for mission building in CAR. It would be a tool for the Polytechnic which Anatole and the *"Nations En Marche"* team were building.

During our final prayer day before the trip, we sensed much warfare and the beginnings of breakthrough. Through prophetic prayer, we overheard the following:

"I am the God of Pygmies and Presidents."

This brought release and encouragement in praying for the destiny of Central African Republic, although I didn't fully grasp all that the Lord was planning.

Armed with this promise and several teaching packs, I left for Charles de Gaulle airport where I was to rendezvous with a Swiss friend who had been a missionary to the Pygmies of Central Africa. His plane from Switzerland was late so I decided to check-in anyway. Imagine my dismay when the lady at the desk kindly informed me that my passport was out of date!

There was no way they would let me travel without a valid passport. I felt so stupid! In my despair, I decided to get all the books and manuals I was carrying out of my bag to pass on to my Swiss friend when he turned up.

"At least they'll be able to arrive," I thought.

As I opened my bag, I saw clothes that were not mine. It slowly dawned on me. By mistake, I had taken the wrong bag from the train! My bag, with the precious cargo of manuals, was probably lost somewhere in Lyon while I had the clothes of some unfortunate holidaymaker!

It was about 11.30 p.m. My ticket was defined as non-refundable! I was also informed that because of the delay of my friend's flight, he had been embarked directly from the runway, so I couldn't even get a message to him. Everything was closed. I began to feel depressed. I wandered into a vacant waiting room to share the floor space with a few lonely, homeless people. I felt so useless! Mocking, evil spirits seemed to be shouting into my downward spiralling thoughts.

"That's the end for you! God's confirming He doesn't want you in Central Africa!"

They mocked the word about the Pygmies and Presidents.

"That's a joke now! An impossibility."

A host of other failures seemed to crowd in on me and I hit rock bottom. I just laid on the floor and cried out to the Lord! It was midnight.

As the hours passed, I felt the Lord gently take hold of my heart. He lifted me out of the pit and raised me to a place of hope and faith, speaking quiet peace into my heart.

"Don't worry. I'll take care of everything."

As it says in the first book of the Bible.

"There was evening, there was morning."

God always takes us from darkness to light - to new beginnings.

And God did take care of everything. He led me to an incredibly helpful railway assistant. She did so much more than duty, and phoned around to trace the missing bag, which they found in Lyon. Usually, I would have had to wait and pay the costs of re-transportation, but she arranged for the bag to be shipped back on the next train to the airport without cost. It would be here by ten o'clock!

Then there was the passport problem. I had two hours to get from the airport to the Swiss consulate in Paris - my passport was Swiss, to see if they would help. It took ages to get there but, wonderfully, they prolonged my passport in a process that took less than fifteen minutes!

And the ticket. Having got my bag and passport sorted, I went to Air France. For an extra £50 they were able to put me on another departure for Bangui, leaving on the Saturday night. My original flight was for Thursday night. I would lose only two days. In the space of three hours, God had worked everything out in a most miraculous way. As I boarded the flight on Saturday night, I felt it was "Resurrection Day!"

Imagine my delight, on arriving in Bangui on Sunday morning, to discover that the congress actually began Monday for a week and not over the week-end as I had wrongly assumed. I had lost nothing by the delay!

After the morning service at brother Anatole's church, *"Fondation Jerusalem,"* we made hectic preparations to travel to the Pygmy conference, which was to be held in the Equatorial forest, some three hours from Bangui. This conference was the fruit of the last year's evangelism. Large groups of Pygmies had come to the Lord through the mission work and many other agencies were now interested in working together. This conference – as all the mission work, was, and still is, totally funded by the Africans themselves. This was the first time such a self-funded conference had ever happened in the country. The delegates either walked or took precarious bush taxis to the venue. About 150 folk were regular attendees at meetings with a total of 360 being present. The conference split between the Pygmy peoples themselves and the agencies seeking to work amongst them.

It was encouraging to see the site the African missionaries had set up, all built by hand from natural resources, costing practically nothing except for the sacrifice of time and sweat. Several mud huts and a meeting hall made up the complex.

Various Pygmy clans gathered around their fires as delegates arrived from different areas of Central African Republic. I'd brought with me a manual tape player equipped with testimonies in the *"Baka"* Pygmy dialect. Although the language wasn't exactly the same as theirs, it was a great ice breaker and the Pygmy families had great fun guessing where the guy on the tape was from. As usual, the millions of mosquitoes, flies and other creepy crawlies also turned up for the conference, no doubt inspired by the promise of fresh white man's blood - a change from the usual routine of Pygmy corpuscles.

The congress began with an all night prayer meeting! Each delegation took an hour, with every session trying to outdo the others in noise and passion. I don't think there was much hope of sleep for those who retired to bed.

Monday began at 5 a.m. with the morning prayer meeting of one hour - night and day tended to blend in such an environment. A couple of hours were given to breakfast and basic washing, before beginning the first service at 8am. Various meetings and workshops took us to 12 am, when a delicious meal of *"boule"* and *"coco"* - prepared from the staple diet of the manioc root, was served. Then we had a siesta till 3pm, teaching till 5.30pm, and then another dose of *"boule"* before an evening session in Pygmy style, including testimony and much dancing around the fire.

Needless to say, all this together made up a beautiful symphony of worship to God and the weeks among the Pygmies were truly a glimpse of heaven on earth, a small corner of paradise.

The pioneer work was established by a great guy called Benjamin Lessy. When I asked him how so many Pygmies had began to follow the Lord since last year, he explained that right at the beginning of their time, one of the Pygmy ladies died. A famous witch doctor - *féticheur*, proclaimed that by his spells he would raise the lady back to life. It was all bluff and he failed. Benjamin felt that this was now an opportunity for him to challenge them that God could raise the dead. He moved out in faith and prayed over the lady, asking God to bring her back to life. The Lord heard his prayer and resurrected the lady! On seeing this incredible miracle, most of the tribe decided that they wanted to follow Jesus. The discipling of a nation – an ethnic tribe, had begun.

Another Pygmy man testified that he had come to the Lord because of the kindness the missionary team had shown him. He had found a wild-boar in his animal trap. Thinking it was dead, he touched the animal which was, however, very much alive! It seriously injured him before escaping. He lay bleeding in the forest. Maggots began to eat away at his wounds. The

Pygmy's wife alerted the mission team who went out to look for him. By the grace of God, they found him and nursed him back to health. He would have died without their intervention.

Another Pygmy man testified with his son. A few months back, his son had broken his leg. The Pygmies have no resources to care for such things and usually the child would have ended up crippled. However, the team were able to send the boy to hospital in Bangui where he was well cared for. He could now walk perfectly. Cheers and hoots rose up from the group as he strutted proudly before us all.

The Pygmies were the earliest inhabitants of Africa. There is something very special about them. From the Biblical verses of Matthew 25, which speak of honouring *"the least - or smallest, of these brothers of mine,"* we sensed that the Pygmy people offered some kind of redemptive opportunity - or the opposite condemnation option, for the Central African Nations.

Their very *vulnerability* was an opportunity for blessing or curse. As we worshipped together, it became apparent that the Bantu people of Central Africa had badly treated the Pygmies and needed to put things right.

A number of folks, representing the various Bantu clans, knelt in tears as they confessed their own sins and the sins of their fathers towards this people. Something seemed to break in the heavenly realms because of these prayers.

The Pygmy worship took on a new dimension and the songs of this particular people seemed to pour blessing and healing afresh on the land. I was thanking the Lord for giving me the opportunity to be a friend to the Pygmies, but as I recalled His promise, I began to doubt whether we would find a President in the midst of the Equatorial forest.

Over the next days, the presence of the Lord was very real. He wanted to lead the nation into a greater measure of healing. At the end of one powerful meeting, unbeknown to many of us previously, a young man stood up. He introduced himself:

"My name is Jean-Serge Bokassa, the son of the former Emperor of Central African Republic."

He explained a dream the Lord had given him. He had seen folks wanting to crown his father. However the crown, although sparkling, was fake gold.

His father's infamous reign – although at first bringing unity, dignity and prosperity to the land, had ended by bringing ruin, violence and repression. The young man explained how difficult it was for him. He wanted to honour the memory of his father and yet, at the same time, own the responsibility for the guilt. He explained how the ancient Emperor had his own sadness. He had been made an orphan after witnessing the murder of his own dad - whipped to death by the colonial rubber barons! He had also witnessed his mother hang herself. Jean-Serge, the son, wanted to ask forgiveness for all the wrongs and evil perpetrated by his father and family.

"I'm sorry, I ask your forgiveness," he said, standing humbly before the assembled groups of Pygmies and Bantus.

The atmosphere became electric as he made this plea for reconciliation. Then gradually, as the Lord led, representatives from each tribal group stood up and forgave, hugging Jean-Serge and exchanging prayers.

One man explained that he was the actual President's cousin, representing the Patassé clan, which was traditionally hostile to Bokassa's. The two men embraced, weeping, forgiving past hurts. Another was struggling to come forward. He finally managed to stand in front of Jean-Serge.

"Your father killed my father," he wept.

Some supernatural force at work within, gave him the strength to forgive. He strode towards Jean-Serge, filled with a miraculous love rather than hate. As he embraced Jean-Serge, the Holy Spirit came down on both men, sending them to the floor. Everyone in the hut was deeply touched and in tears. It was a very profound moment. A brother from Cameroon felt led to anoint the very soil with oil as a sign of the deep healing that the Lord had done through the prayers of reconciliation.

As this was going on, a mighty thunder storm tore open the heavens and the rain came pouring down. It was a moving, majestic moment. Words alone do not do the scene justice. As the rain washed the land, I was reminded of the prophetic word that God had spoken.

"I am the God of Pygmies and Presidents."

I felt so privileged to have had some part in it all.

A few years later, at the end of 2003, the nation was in the midst of a national conference for reconciliation, held in their Houses of Parliament, with the proceedings being broadcast nationwide. Presidents and former Presidents were together trying to find a way forward. Suddenly, the protocol was shattered when a young man stood up and gave his own personal testimony of reconciliation that had occurred a few years back in the forest. The man was Jean-Serge Bokassa and his intervention brought a strategic breakthrough which led to bitter political opponents publicly asking forgiveness of one another. The meeting concluded with all the delegations chanting:

"We want prayer! We want prayer!"

In the light of this, I tend to believe that God can change a nation from the bottom up, and that He is indeed the God of Pygmies and Presidents. As I am writing up these memories many years later, it is interesting to note that Jean-Serge will be standing for election as President of Central African Republic at the end of 2015. Watch this space!

I'll end this long session on Africa, with a further story of new beginnings from my time in the Equatorial jungle. This took place during the festive season and is a Christmas tale from the forest.

Just how many people can you cram into a Mitsubishi Pajero ?

On the average trip to the Bobelé Pygmy encampment in Central African Republic the answer may take on an entirely different dimension. For a start, you have to pack the vehicle full with as many bananas, yams, and other cut price delicacies from the generous forest. Myself, as the honoured guest, is then ensconced in glory in the front seat with Anatole Banga's two children, Ariel and Caleb. The next row is filled with Anatole himself, his wife Odile, Benjamin Lessy our pioneer African missionary to these Pygmies, and a very pregnant African lady called Opportune. And, just when you were already holding your breath for lack of air and pressure, five Pygmies are squeezed in for good measure! Of course, you also need to include the driver in the grand total of *thirteen*.

As we bounced along the forest tracks, a mobile fount of plenty, I couldn't help but doubt the beautiful image of solitude generated by the pictures of Mary and Joseph as they travel along to Bethlehem on a slightly less than loaded donkey.

The wheels dipped violently into the thousandth pot-hole in the track as a muffled cry emerged from the heavily pregnant lady next to Anatole. Through gritted teeth, the cries grew louder as the labour pains came in unstoppable waves. It's one thing to pray to be the *"father"* of many nations, but we were on the verge of experiencing the only too real consequences of new birth.

The Pygmies stared, Anatole grew paler by the minute, the lady groaned and bananas flew in all directions as the driver headed full speed for the capital city of Bangui. We arrived at a small set of buildings which served as a maternity ward in the aptly named area called *"Bimbo."* We carried the lady out of the car and gratefully handed her over to what the French call *"sage femmes"* - wise women, or midwives for the English.

Two minutes later, a shrill cry broke the hot, humid African air as the miracle of new life was welcomed into the world. A cloud, obscuring the evening sun, permitted sun beams to stream out of heaven as God seemed to be giving his own particular welcome to this precious African child. My own eyes filled with tears at the majesty of the moment.

Two thousand years ago, another cry broke the middle eastern skies above Bethlehem. A cry no less human - yet divinely redemptive, as God became a man to live, suffer and die amongst us. A cry that brought life and forgiveness to untold millions around the world, drawing the rich and the poor together in worship and causing God to fling a new star into space.

This Christmas adventure was yet another chapter in my history with Central African Republic. While the Embassies were withdrawing their staff and closing, and while the missionaries were leaving because of the political instability and anarchy, we felt we should be holding a mass rally for reconciliation and change in the nation. Standing shoulder to shoulder with brothers in their hour of need does more good than a year of sermons.

Miraculously, the Lord opened the door for us to hold a three day period of fasting, prayer and repentance for all the pastors and church leaders. The government enabled us to use their parliament buildings for this free of charge. Only the bravest pastors turned up for this event - about a hundred folk, but we had a critical mass of faith to be able to intercede prophetically for the nation.

This was followed by a mass rally in front of the national stadium where over two thousand people gathered to pray and take part in a reconciliation ceremony which involved the various tribes and factions asking forgiveness of one another.

It has been an ongoing privilege of my life to have been able to teach the students at Anatole's Polytechnic for many years, along with several other gifted teachers and men of God who have come alongside to lend a hand. Continual, fervent prayer has been the lifeblood of this work. In spite of facing successive coups and violence, shocking poverty and breakdown of society - and even resistance from the established church, the first wave of missionaries were already successfully graduating in April 2003. The world is not worthy of such as these. Since then, many other students have followed them right up to this present day.

The work in Bobelé continued to grow with whole areas being cultivated and earning a living for the missionaries. The indigenous Pygmy church has also grown and, at the end of one particular Sunday service, a young Pygmy mother presented me with her new baby girl, wanting me to give her a name. I named her *Sylviane*, after my wife, which means *"daughter of the forest."*

A dispensary has been established and has been instrumental in saving many lives. An educational programme has also brought dignity and progress to many.

This is the holistic gospel. God's Shalom !

Sadly, the Pygmy encampment with the school and medical work were recently attacked in the 2014 -15 violence that has once again overrun the land. Many of the Pygmies had to run for shelter into the forest for several weeks. The work survived and, in spite of the opposition, it seems that God does indeed have a wonderful destiny for this nation. Recent research has uncovered the biggest oil reserves in the world under this country's earth, which may explain some of the political unrest at the moment.

God came to man, born amongst muck and beasts in a violent, poverty stricken world. His Shalom became flesh.

In front of *"Bimbo's"* maternity shacks, a small new born baby girl was carried out for me to bless. Fragile, stained with blood - yet covered in the white sheen of the new-born, she seemed to symbolise all that Central Africa could be in the future. I remembered Saul's blessing of David and prayed:

"May you be blessed, my daughter; you will do great things and surely triumph."

They also named her a daughter of the forest.

14 Redeeming the Dreams

Having taken you on a journey to the nations, it's time to come back to France. For over 20 years, I had the joy of being part of a small, slow burn miracle that is being worked out in the north of France. A miracle, conceived in the prophetic destiny of God, and yet carried and birthed in the simple prayers and perseverance of ordinary men and women willing to give their all, take risks and abandon themselves to grace and purpose.

The physical substance of this miracle is a beautiful 16th century white castle - *"Le Château Blanc,"* but the invisible part is the substance of faith, which, in creating a secure foundation of intercession, has brought, and will continue to bring, hope and redemption to France and the nations.

Sacrificial service and selfless giving of time and money have wrought a spiritual credibility into the ministry which is reproducing itself as mission movements of quality men and women in French speaking Africa and beyond. Many are beginning to come to know Christ in the village of Thumeries which has cradled the Château Blanc building for many decades. The ministry of the Gospel has been able to cut across the historic boundaries which have often kept Protestants and Catholics apart and, as I rejoiced at the growing hunger for Jesus - reflected in the recent baptism of a local lady who discovered the Lord through contact with the Château team, I sensed that this village, along with many others in France, is ripe for spiritual revival.

Martin Luther King started his own miracle of reconciliation with a dream.

"I have a dream."

Our own story also starts with a dream.

Many years ago, the German wife of a French Baptist pastor - who headed up a growing church in the town of Roubaix, had a God given dream of a white castle. She saw a big wooden fireplace and a traditional Flemish style stepped down roof. At this time, they discovered a château at Thumeries which was being put on the market by members of the Béghin family. *Béghin-Say* was a multinational sugar company in France which is now known as the *Tereos* group. Their family had strongly influenced France in many ways. Thumeries was a kind of modern 'feudal' town, revolving around their factory where 5000 used to be employed. The sons and daughters of Mr. Béghin married influential bankers and traders. One of the most famous sons was the world renowned film director, Louis Malle, whose films included *"Au Revoir les Enfants,"* a tale of the persecution of Jews during the wartime Vichy regime in France.

The Château has a long history going back to at least 1547, which is a date inscribed in one of the stones and backed up by local history. Thumeries may also have its roots from the Celtic word Tumulus - meaning burial mound, although this is unsure. The original builders were Spanish knights, the Hamaide family. Other important owners were the Baron de Carondelet and a bishop who renounced his faith during the persecution of the French revolution. Both Germans and the allies occupied the Chateau during the war years.

At the time of the dream, the Baptist church at Roubaix had strong links with another Baptist church in Essen, Germany - this church took over an infamous, old 'Krupps' building to use for their church. One lady in this church had a very strong prophetic gifting. Without any correspondence with France, she also had a dream and saw a Château that she felt would be for the future work. She stipulated that God had shown her a place with water around it and red gravel on the path. Imagine the conviction they must have had when they gathered at the Château to see red gravel and a moat running around the building. The lady picked up a handful of the red gravel and said:

"This place is for the Lord!"

They planned a joint project together to purchase the Château with a view to running some kind of training school.

However, the Béghin family met together to discuss the proposal. At the end of the family meeting, old father Béghin made the following vow:

"We are Catholics and will never sell this property to Protestants. Our son Patrick was killed by Germans in Paris at the end of the 2nd world war, and we will never sell to anything which involves Germans!"

Nothing would change their minds, so it seemed that all the leading and prophetic dreams had been a mistake.

Daniel - the pastor from Roubaix, was leading a charismatic renewal in the Baptist church at the time. He was questioned concerning the validity of the prophetic revelation through these events. In the face of a closed door, they simply prayed, committing the vision back to God.

The castle was then sold to a man who had won some money in the National Lottery. A sad period began for the place. All the water pipes burst one winter while the owner was away. He sold off the farm part of the Château as a separate unit, thus reducing access to the property. There is a small wood belonging to the Château. In a shady deal, he planned to convert this wood into building land. Despite a petition from the village, he proceeded to cut down all of the large 500 year old oak trees. The wood was decimated and never even sold as building land. No upkeep was made on the building.

The physical destruction mirrored a spiritual evil as well. At the time when I first began visiting the Château, I was surprised to be greeted by a man-sized Buddha at the entrance. In every single room, hideous idols from many different countries of the world had been set up. Cupboards contained Chinese death masks. For what was explained as *"decorative purposes,"* there were human skulls and witch-like dolls on the tables. The owner's wife was a very mysterious, sad, dark looking lady. Even in the time we were involved, violent storms lashed the property, causing roof damage and several trees to be uprooted. It seemed as if the destructive forces of evil were intent on thwarting whatever prophetic purposes lay behind the acquiring of this building for the Lord's work.

However, God is a God of redemption and, even as ten long years passed from that initial dream, the prophetic root was simply getting ready to send another green shoot bursting out from this seemingly dry ground. While leading a meeting at our base in the Ardèche Valley, and without the slightest knowledge of the previous *"Château"* story or dream, I heard a word which was to change the direction of my life for the next twenty years. The worship rose heavenwards and a prophetic word was given concerning a building in the North of France. A rather scruffy young man blurted out:

"The Lord wants to give you a "Château Blanc" in this region."

We had been praying about expanding our work to the North of France and had a few links there via a close friend and his welcome ministry to groups passing through the area. I was due to spend time with him along with the leader of our mission. I remember chatting with him about the prophecy I had recently received.

"Oh. You need to be careful about prophecies and weigh everything up," came his wise counsel.

As he finished speaking, the phone rang. To my surprise, it was from the very man who had given the prophecy a couple of weeks previously. An excited, out of breath voice blurted out the following story.

"You'll never guess what Rob. I was hitch-hiking, when a man stopped to pick me up. I got into his car and he immediately began to speak to me about a white Château that he was looking to sell. He leant over to me and, half joking said, "You don't want to buy a Château do you?" I said "No," but then gave him your name!"

"What an amazing co-incidence," I thought, as I put the phone down.

That same afternoon, we had a visit from Daniel Lhermenault - the French Baptist pastor, who proceeded to share with us his story concerning the Château.

My friend who had given the prophecy had taken the phone number of the man who was selling a Château, so I phoned him up to arrange a visit, wondering if this could possibly be the same Château that Daniel's wife had dreamt about all those years ago.

The building was situated in Thumeries, and, as we approached the town, we could see a stepped down Flemish roof, a moat and red gravel! Was this the time for the Château to come back into the Lord's purposes?

As we looked around the place, there was a feeling of rightness - and yet an enormous challenge of renovation and financial outlay. Logically, it would not have been sensible to buy the place in view of the work, but it seemed that God wanted someone to stand in the gap and take up the baton of His purpose which had been laid down previously.

Daniel shared with us how the Lord had showed him three candlesticks burning in the North of France - one represented England, one France, and one Germany. He felt these three lands should be coming together in reconciliation to bless Europe.

The building was priced at £180,000 with about £20,000 more in taxes. We had no immediate finance available. There was also a major concern about the fire regulations for such a public building and the access route for a fire engine. New bridges would have to be built and the future work would be enormous and sacrificial.

The pressure on me to make a decision about buying the Château became very heavy and I found myself ill with bronchitis. Although folks are often very enthusiastic to give some prophetic message or direction, there is often less enthusiasm when it comes down to owning the consequences of such a revelation – particularly when that revelation may involve financial and personal sacrifice! As I lay in bed, I decided to listen to some teaching cassettes.

One speaker spoke about how he thought that the Welsh revival should have ushered in a world revival of religion, but that the enemy had thwarted that through the First World War. So many of the young, heroic and innocent soldiers were massacred in the *"killing fields"* of Northern France. Europe was buzzing at the turn of the century as the Holy Spirit visited his people. The Welsh revival released a generation of men and women on fire for God and world evangelisation - 100,000 souls were saved in 6 months! In 1910, the Edinburgh conference on World Evangelisation was held and hopes were high. Rick Ridings, a prominent intercessor for Europe, wrote about this:

"Many Christian historians feel that Europe was prepared for revival around 1900. Many Christian student movements were experiencing great growth and a vision for world missions and the re-evangelisation of Europe. Just at that time, regional tensions in the Balkans, flared into World War 1. Two of the countries with the most young men called into mission - Germany and Great Britain, ended up sending these young men into battle against one another."

The dreams of so many young men died on the battlefields of Northern France. As I contemplated these truths, I distinctly heard the Holy Spirit whisper these words into my spirit.

"Redeem the Dreams."

I felt God calling me and the team, through prayer and sacrificial lifestyle, to raise up a place of redemptive power where a new generation of men and women could take up the lost dreams, and so fulfil their destiny in God's purposes.

Men came from the four corners of the world to die. Why shouldn't a new generation be raised up from the ends of the earth to bring resurrection life and promise to the nations.

I remembered our mission leader telling me how he used to travel to the North of France with a Welsh evangelist. In his spare moments, he would climb up to Vimy Ridge - a key battlefield and now a Canadian memorial to the War dead, to pray. Overlooking the fields of carnage, where unexploded bombs still remain dormant and where farmers regularly discover the bones of long dead soldiers as they till their fields, a prayer would rise, inspired from the prophet Ezekiel's cry:

"Can these bones live again?"

We began praying for this new generation to go out into the world from here with the message of life. In chapter 37 of the book of Ezekiel in the Bible , the vision ends with the resurrection of a nation and *"a vast army"* on their feet. I felt that, in some mysterious way, the buying and renovation of the Château would be significant for the mobilising of such an army. The Lord then whispered the Biblical words of the prophet Haggai – chapter 2 verse 9, into my heart.

"In this place I will bring peace."

"If this is all from you Lord," I prayed, lungs wheezing, as I lay sick in bed.

"Let me be given this very same verse as I go into the prayer meeting this morning."

I made an effort to get out of my sick bed, dressed and joined the regular Thursday prayer time which was being held at our base in Bourg St Andéol.

"Does anyone have a word for me I asked?"

Immediately, a lady read out with faith and authority.

"In this place I will bring peace."

The Château project was undertaken in that holy moment.

The financial reality was still a very real challenge. I, in my own disorganised way, must have been the worst qualified person to take on such a project. The harder I pushed to get people and churches to give, the less money seemed to come in! In the end, I abandoned myself to prayer and fasting, spending long hours in prayer on the banks of the Rhone river, finding inspiration from Rees Howells book *"Intercessor"* and his testimonies of how he prayed in the money for the Bible College of Wales.

I was no Rees Howells, but the Lord graciously led us through against impossible odds. Quite extraordinarily, a bank was brave enough to loan us £100,000 without guarantees, while friends generously gave us interest free loans. I remember emptying my pockets on the last day, giving all I had and doing my maths on the back of an old piece of paper. We had just enough to scrape through, plus thirty seven francs!

Our rejoicing over the victory was tempered by the very real sense of a battle only just beginning. We had no furniture, no tools and a virtually nonexistent electric system in the building.

The initial mission team at the Château was made up of English, Belgian and Germans. We started with a large evangelistic campaign, involving over 100 folk covering Lille, Roubaix and other areas. In the first year, there was a constant stream of visitors, pushing resources to their limit. Things seemed to be going well, with us making steps in paying off the loan.

Then things went less well. Blocked sewage pipes meant that wastewater was overflowing into the moat, killing off all the fish and making a rotten smell.

Team unity began to suffer and, very quickly, destructive elements seemed to be finding their way back in through division. Both the physical and spiritual fabric of the place continued to suffer. Much credit must be given to the perseverance of the leadership - those early pioneers, at this time of testing. The local fire safety officer brought a team round the place to inspect our installations. It was a time when we had groups everywhere, sleeping on floors, stairs and corridors. Dangerous electric wires dangled down the walls and ceilings in a hungry quest to find the available sockets that worked. The fire officer was not impressed and immediately closed the building due to the danger it represented through lack of modern fire installations. This meant us being faced with even higher renovation costs, the bank loan to pay and no resources coming in from groups.

The situation seemed impossible. It was at this time that we began to sense the need to pray specifically in and around the château. At one session, with folks from Britain, we felt we needed to release the house from the curse of 'blood-guilt'. This was related to Nazism and the Hindu gods behind it. We needed specifically to release the house from the hold of the 'dead son' from the Béghin family. We also prayed out the past and were led in various prophetic actions in the building.

Following this, God brought new folks to help in the building and leadership. One such blessing were the Miller family. James Miller was an engineer and surveyor - the ideal person to help us get the building back on track. I often used to wonder how God could call a successful engineer to move from the security of a job and a good life in Sevenoaks to the risky life of faith the Château offered. I think James also wondered at times! A measure of answer came in an old book that James received from his Grandma which spoke about the wartime exploits of his Grandfather's regiment in France. In one account, it spoke of them walking over a bridge near Henin Beaumont on the way to a village called Thumeries. The account went on saying how they were lodged in the village Château! Without James knowing it, his Grandfather had stayed in the same Château that he had been called by God to help renovate.

The sense of destiny and the call to redeem something from the tragic loss of the First World War grew through such memorable stories. James helped us build a new bridge over the moat. Here was a man who had a key role in building the Copenhagen Underground, used to an unlimited budget and professional contractors, having to work with the willing amateurs and volunteers of the Château team. I well remember one work team introducing themselves to James. One was over seventy, the second had a bad heart and the third had only one arm – and yet what sterling servants they turned out to be! Another German group, who enthusiastically volunteered to climb ladders and go on roofs, turned out to have a number of seriously disturbed drug addicts whose grip on reality was often limited.

"As long as they don't think they can fly," James joked, as we climbed the high ladders.

We found ourselves continually locked up with God in prayer with many being led into intensive periods of fasting. Humanly, there was no way out, but we felt that, through the pressure, God was calling us to Himself, wanting to lay a true foundation of faith and dependence upon Him alone. During this time, we felt we needed to break every ancient curse over the château and take it into the place of blessing to which it was destined.

Many folks felt keenly that we should also be praying into the areas of colonial domination by the lands of Britain, France and Germany. That somehow, we should redeem the exploitation of these lands - especially the French speaking ones, from slavery.

As we engaged in such a prayer purpose, we found ourselves led in ministry to the Central African Republic – the previous chapters have given you a glimpse of how our prayers literally incarnated themselves in this land, playing our part in raising up an African army for world mission. Several African brothers have become regular visitors to the ministry in Thumeries. It is stunning to think that the tragic genocides in Rwanda and other African nations - revival turning into destruction and death, mirrors what happened in the Welsh revival - the powers of destruction through the First World War being unleashed to kill a potential army for world evangelisation.

However, we serve a God of resurrection and life, so death certainly doesn't have the last word, and is only God's stepping-stone into ultimate victory and celebration.

In October 1994, the Lord met with us in a very special way. Finance and bills had always been a slightly less than joyful experience for me, and I would carry around unpaid bills in my pockets like wounds. We'd pray and eventually battle our way through to answer, but we grew weary and worried from the heavy financial burden. It was a season of refreshing in the Church and many were experiencing deep renewal from the move of God which originated in Toronto. One of my colleagues came back from such a meeting in Britain and, when I saw him, I could see a new peace and lightness on his face.

"What's happened to you?" I said.

"God met with me in a new way," he replied.

"Do you want me to pray for you?"

Up till then, I had been quietly cynical about this new move of God and its weird manifestations, but I felt I should lay my prejudices aside and give it a go. He gently laid his hands on me and began to pray. Before I knew it, I was face down on the floor, laughing like some demented chicken! Sweat was running down my face and, as I lay sprawled out on the floor in front of my team, I thought:

"I'm losing my dignity in front of everyone."

But God's word suddenly broke in with this reply.

"Oh no. It's not your dignity that you are losing, only your pride !"

The laughter was like some profound healing intercession which went deep into the soul. Just as the sterile Sara was able to birth an Isaac - he laughs, from her dead womb and unbelieving heart, so God, through the waves of laughter, was pouring in fresh faith and fruitfulness to my own tired spirit. The worry and burden of the finances seemed to lift. I even found myself looking at the water and rates bills that were in my pockets and laughing out loud over them. Now that really was a miracle! When was the last time you laughed over your bills?

We went throughout the Château building, laughing and worshipping in every room. It was like a spiritual Spring cleaning, kicking out the old sadness and welcoming in the new joy. The Lord locked us into a discipline of laughter. For about two weeks, we could not pray about finances without hysterical laughter breaking out amongst us. Needless to say, the Lord faithfully met our needs, but more than that, we had fallen in love again with the Giver rather than getting bogged down by the needs and service. For me, that time was a deliverance from the bondage to worry and burden over finances, and, in spite of many new challenges in that area, I have been able to see through projects with a new faith and lightness of spirit.

As one of the last payments on the Château, we needed to repay an interest free loan of £30,000. I was staying on the Isle of Man at a youth camp when news came through that the planned route of repayment had failed and that we needed the money in the next five days. It was indeed a challenge. I can still remember walking around Ramsey dock side at daybreak, looking out to sea and talking to the seals about the issue. Their quiet stares were a real encouragement! The Lord gently said to me from Psalm 46:6:

"God is within her she will not fall;
God will help her at break of day."

Indeed, God did help in an amazing way which enabled the loan to be paid off within the five day limit. At this present time, the Château is fully paid for, fully equipped, fulfilling all the French fire security rules, and growing into its role as a comfortable residential centre for folks to discover prayer and mission. A new leadership team is in place and a new generation are discovering the joy of redeeming their dreams...and scraping walls!

We had the privilege of playing a significant role in launching a powerful nation-wide prayer push over a number of years. We ran a non-stop 40 day prayer vigil, 24 hours a day, over the Lent period which planted a peg of intercession into the French speaking world which will not be easily removed. Since that time, France and our works in French speaking Africa, have experienced very positive changes in the spiritual climate and the political arena. During the first prayer push, a prophetic word was given by a lady who knew nothing of our past dealings. The Lord put the following words on her heart:

"Many intercessors have prayed for the battlefields of France - rightfully so. The Lord never forgets where blood has been shed. I saw the beautifully kept cemeteries of Northern France. Each white cross had poppies on it but then when I looked again, it seemed that there was an army on the move. It seemed that a new army of young people was on the move, men and women. They were very serious about their task but at the same time, there was a great joy in them. They marched from across the sea into France where they met together and became an army. They marched into the cemeteries and took up the crosses. At first it looked rather shocking but each young person took up a white cross and put it across their own shoulder before marching on right across Europe. I could not see any obvious leader in charge or any order having been given. No words even were being spoken, yet they all knew exactly what they were doing and why. It seemed as if there was a redemptive value in this act, and that the lives lost in the past were going to be honoured in a way no man could ever do, no matter how well the memory of the past is honoured. These lives were going to be of value in the future in battles not yet fought.

There was a beautiful sense of the Lord redeeming time and apparent waste of lives in the past. There was a joy and a solemnity about the scene which was quite remarkable. I did not see where the young people ended up. There were several destinations in Europe, and I knew they would get there and do more than those who had given their lives in the two great wars this century. The task would be more than completed."

What a marvellous encouragement it was to see the Lord, all these years later, taking us back to the original vision of *"Redeeming the Dreams."* We have seen young people from Africa and Korea training at the Château as well as being a source of prayer and inspiration for many local French churches and Christians. Volunteer groups, armed with prayers and paint brushes, continue to give valuable help as well as receive revelation and encouragement for their own missionary vision.

Hundreds have also been reached through different evangelistic enterprises – notably the work of *"En Route Ensemble,"* which was founded at the Château and which mobilises the church in the North to street evangelism, using barbecues to contact folk. Dynamic cell groups, English language courses and a post-Alpha gathering in Thumeries, regularly gather folk to prayer and fellowship.

And the dreams continue! As a young girl, one of my Franco/African colleagues - Maguy Barthaburu, dreamt prophetically of all that the Lord would do over a number of years in her nation of Central African Republic. This lead her into a life of deep intercession. She married a Basque Frenchman born in Algeria – Jean, and, after a time in Africa, they found themselves in a Bible School in Denmark. During their time there, the Lord clearly showed Maguy the Château Blanc in a dream and told them that this was to be the next step for their ministry. They then heard about our work by chance as they were passing through, visiting friends in the North. They made their way to the Château and found it to be all that Maguy had seen in her dream – except for one detail. She had seen a decorated Château and we were in the midst of redecoration. We had already chosen our colour scheme and decided to test Maguy's dream by asking her which colours the Château was decorated in. She had 250 options to choose from. Amazingly, she chose the right colours!

From that moment, they felt a strong call to join the Château ministry. They have done amazing works over the years and have both developed influential ministries, taking up the baton of prayer and intercession. A few years ago, Jean felt led to serve as the leader of the team. He has been joined by an enthusiastic group from Korea and a number of quality French Christians.

A short while ago, in the wake of all the violence that was happening in Central African Republic, a reconciliation meeting - sponsored by the French Foreign Office, was held at the Château. The local mayor was invited to give an introduction. I nearly fell off my chair when he opened his speech by quoting the famous words from Martin Luther King.

"I have a dream."

He then went on to say how much he appreciated the Evangelical values of the Château team.

There are so many unsung heroes in this story. So many came to serve and welcome, cook and clean, pray and worship, love and preach. They were willing to do the hard, hidden, ordinary jobs. Each one has a special place in my heart and represents a life sown in service.

As we go through our different seasons of the vision, we can look back over the past and say a big *"Ebenezer"* – the Lord has indeed been our *"Stone of Help"* as we've played our part in looking after this big stone in the North of France. Jacob anointed his stone, which was a place of communication with heaven, the very house of God.

May the Lord keep us flexible and anointed as we pursue our dreams and try to build an environment where others, like us, can find their dream becoming a reality.

And ultimately, like the prophet Daniel in chapter 2 verse 23 of the Bible, may we also be able to say that we have been an expression of that ultimate dream, the dream of King Jesus, to see a global Bride making herself ready for eternity.

"You have made known to us the dream of the king."

15 The White House

After the adventures of *"Le Château Blanc,"* you may also be interested in a more personal story concerning, *"La Maison Blanche"* - the white house.

After many years of living a community and nomadic lifestyle, I had never thought of getting a home for my own family. When we moved to the north, to spearhead the Château project, it was our third move in two years and we were able to put all the worldly goods of a five member family into the back of a small Ford Transit van.

Our aim was to stay in the Château, but, as the place had been closed down for fire security reasons, we found ourselves camping in one ground floor meeting room. The circumstances pushed me to ask the Lord about future accommodation prospects. One day, as I was reading through the Bible, the following words of God to King David struck me.

"The Lord declares to you that the Lord himself will establish a house for you."
2 Samuel 7:11

I then found myself at a conference in Bordeaux which was concerned with building up networks throughout the French speaking world. At the end of one session, I was approached by my friends and colleagues, Garry and Pam, who were then strengthening the base at Bourg St Andéol in the Ardèche. Without knowing of our situation, Pam said to me.

"I felt the Lord telling me that he wanted to give you a house."

She added that I should not minimise God's ability to provide. What she didn't tell me - because of her wisdom in not wanting to pressurise me to an agenda, was that God had clearly told her that I was to have the house within a week! She told this only to her husband at the time and they made a record of this revelation. I'm glad that she was wise enough not to tell me as I had a hard enough job just believing God for the house itself.

I returned that Monday night and shared the encouragement with my wife Sylviane. We decided to take an evening walk around the village and see if there were any signs of houses to rent.

"Our problem ," I said to Sylviane.

"Is that we are newcomers to this area and don't have the local contacts who could lead us to the right places."

I then stopped in front of an imposing looking house and continued:

"This house for example. We don't even know if something like this might be up for rent or not. Many folks have told me that it's virtually impossible to rent in a village like this, and we've no money to buy."

We then went home, challenged to believe God's word rather than the less than promising circumstances. The following day, I visited the local Estate Agent in the next village and asked them if they had anything to rent in Thumeries. The lady there explained that renting in Thumeries was a rarity and that even houses to buy were getting harder to find.

"However, you might be interested in this house that has just come on the market in Thumeries," she uttered hopefully, showing us a picture of a big white house which was the very building we had paused in front of the night before.

We agreed to make a visit. The house was quite run down, but sound. It had three bedrooms, a large attic for two more, and the most wonderful walled garden which contained a beautiful apple tree.

We loved the place and felt that this would indeed be the ideal home for us. However, we also felt that we were walking in fantasy land as we came to terms with the fact that this house was only for sale and that we didn't have any money. I dared to ask anyway.

"How much does the owner want for this house?"

"It's on the market for 470.000 FF plus tax."

That was about £47,000 at the time, and way beyond anything we could envisage. We thanked the lady and made our way back to our one room at the Château.

"It's good to dream," I said, having decided, through fear and unbelief - under the disguise of common sense, that this house was not for us.

The Wednesday morning, I awoke and needed to travel to the next village. As I passed the Estate Agent's, an inner intuition seemed to give me a new faith and boldness, as I remembered my friends' words about not limiting God's ability to provide. Some unseen hand seemed to guide me into the offices and I could scarcely believe my ears as I heard myself saying.

"I would like to make an offer of 400.000 FF - about £40,000, for the house we visited yesterday."

The lady asked me to put the offer in writing and explained that it was a serious business to make such an offer, and that I would be informed of the outcome the next day. When I got home to Sylviane, I was a bit shell shocked.

"I may have done a stupid thing," I said.

"If he accepts our offer, where will we find £40,000? No bank in their right mind would give a loan to someone with no salary or security to offer. I've not even properly looked around the house or had it surveyed!"

I went to bed a worried man, almost wishing to be let off the hook by a refusal of our offer. The Thursday was our team prayer day, so it was in an atmosphere of praise and worship that the phone rang with the Estate Agent on the other end of the phone.

"Mr Reeve, your offer has been accepted and you will need to sign the official contract – le compromis de vente, at the solicitor's tomorrow morning, bringing a down payment of 10% of the price."

I hung up not knowing whether to be pleased or petrified!

The immediate challenge was for £4,000. I decided to be bold and shameless and rang my parents to ask if they could lend me £5,000 and put it into my bank account straight away! It wasn't easy for them, but with the promise of certain re-imbursement, they agreed. Amazingly, I was also to receive gifts, and squeezing dry every possible source of personal finance, I managed to raise another £5,000!

Encouraged by this provision, I went with confidence that afternoon to a bank in Lille to ask for a loan of £30,000. This bank was linked to the bank I had just left in the Ardèche, and I hoped that they would be sympathetic as I had banked with their group for a number of years. I felt intimidated by the smooth, professional atmosphere of the bank and felt very much out of place. A sophisticated lady received me.

"Well Mr Reeve, what can we do for you?"

"I'd like a loan to buy a house," I replied.

The basic details were shared and we got to the delicate question of what I did for a living. To my shame, I felt threatened by the secular environment, and didn't have the courage to state clearly the evangelical element of my missionary vocation.

"I work for a Christian humanitarian organisation," I said, trying to make a good impression.

"Oh, very nice. What is your salary?" came the reply.

I felt stupid as I bumbled out something about not receiving a regular salary, but living by the generosity of friends and churches.

"You are joking! Mr Reeve?" enquired the lady incredulously, and with a certain amount of disdain in her voice.

She realised that I was indeed serious and, no doubt because of my weak compromise about my faith, shot back at me the following withering statement.

"You must be mad to think anyone would give you a loan without you having a salaried job and pay slips to hand. You are ridiculous. You can leave now."

I was rudely shown the door and I left, vanquished and crestfallen.

Back home, I shut myself into prayer with God. Firstly, I repented for my lack of boldness concerning my work and also for the fear of man which had gripped me. It was at that moment, feeling welcomed by grace into the presence of God, that I seemed to overhear the following directions in my spirit.

The Lord appeared to be saying that He forgave my weakness, but that he wanted me to testify boldly for him in the local bank of Thumeries. This bank belonged to the group, *"Crédit Agricole,"* and I had never even set foot in one of their agencies before. I felt the Lord's leading to ask to see the bank manager. Before leaving, the Lord advised me to wear a tie for the meeting.

I walked into the bank and asked to see the manager who just happened to be available. He welcomed me into his office and, as we were about to sit down, I launched into a bold declaration.

"I'm a Christian and I love Jesus Christ. I work as a missionary, sharing my hope in the resurrection of Christ. I do not receive any salary but trust God to provide for all my needs through the Church."

Seeing that he hadn't yet kicked me out, I added for good measure.

"And I would like to buy a house in Thumeries and need a £30,000 loan."

He seemed slightly in shock by my sudden outburst and, in an attempt to bring the conversation back to a more terrestrial foundation, he asked me:

"Which house are you thinking of buying?"

"The one in Rue Gambetta. Number eleven." I replied.

"Well, that's interesting. I was also after that house, but, in the end, my wife chose somewhere else. It has a nice garden. How much did you offer?"

How amazing. This man had been after the same house. A certain rapport was created because of this and I was simply overwhelmed when he said to me.

"I like what you do. I will do all I can to make sure that you get your loan of £30,000."

So when Friday morning came, I was able to sign the contract with the promise of the loan to pay the final *"acte de vente"* in six weeks, when we would be moving in. As the ink of my signature dried on the crisp document, I realised that it had taken from Monday to Friday to buy a house! It was only a couple of months later, when we had already moved in, that I had a visit from Garry and Pam who then joyously shared how God had given them the revelation of the 'one week' time definition of the prophetic word!

The adventure went on as the couple who were occupying the house didn't look like moving out in time for our coming in. I went to see them the day before our move to let them know we were coming. He owned a little lorry and was willing to let us use it to move our stuff in, while he then took his stuff out. It was a real nightmare, with chairs, tables and all sorts of objects flying in every direction, but we finally got there in the end.

Under French law, for many years until I handed over the responsibility, I was known as *"Le Président"* of *"Le Château Blanc."* It was only natural for the President to live in the White House!

This house has proved a real haven for our family over the years, and has also been a place of prayer and welcome. We were indeed able to welcome the wonderful gift of our fourth child, Myriam – our little northern *Ch'ti*, into its warm security and blessing.

I often think back to that early word, given at my commissioning service at the Anglican Church, which spoke about buildings and temples. With my white castle and white house I'm no match for Solomon, but I hope, at least in some small way, that the Lord may always find a home – not just in our buildings, but in our hearts.

"The one whom God has chosen is young and inexperienced. The task is great, because this palatial structure is not for man but for the Lord God." 1 Chronicles 29:1

16 China Calling

Way back in November 2000, I remember seeing a programme on French television concerning the First World War. It was about how the Chinese - allies to the British and French, sent over hundreds of men to help dig the trenches in the North of France. A whole village was used to billet these men who brought their Chinese traditions as well as their opium addiction - a sad legacy left by the British imperialism in China. Most of them died, not in battle, but due to the cold and influenza that they caught while digging the trenches. A lonely forgotten monument still stands to them in a farmer's field.

As I had been pursuing, for a number of years, the vision to 'redeem the dreams' of all that was lost through the First World War, this vision of something to redeem from China sowed quite a prayer burden in my heart. For a number of days, I began to pray more for China. Imagine my delight, when in early December 2000, a colleague rang me up and asked if I would like to go to China with him. He wanted me to be able to leave within the following ten days! Despite creating some disruption to my schedule, it was an offer I couldn't refuse.

I began to pray and read up on the culture and history of China. I found out how much the thinking of the ancients - men like Lao-Tzu and Confucius, had had a major influence on forming the Chinese world view. In a nutshell, both were concerned with explaining the eternal order, known as *"Tao."*

Lao-Tzu saw the Tao as manifested in nature. Confucius' eye saw it more expressed through humanity and social relationships. Confucius emphasised the past and its wisdom, while Lao-Tzu emphasised the present experience.

God, it seems, is always at work in any culture, preparing an environment to receive the beautiful revelation of Christ into every appropriate cultural context. Indeed, the Chinese translation of Christ's statement in John 14:6:

"I am the way," is, *"I am the Tao."*

I was also struck by the way recent history had modelled the nation and, having lived in France for many years - the home of the great *"Sun King"* Louis Quatorze, I was particularly interested in the influence of the *"Versailles Treaty."*

After having been on the allies side - albeit briefly and no doubt for political reasons, the Chinese were hoping to regain the territory that the Germans had taken over. At this time, the eyes of the youth and intelligentsia of China were very much looking to the West for a model of society.

Woodrow Wilson, the American President at the time, for fear of being manipulated, conceded the German conquests of China to the Japanese instead of giving them back to China. This was seen as a gross betrayal of China by the West, and emphasised the idea of the *"foreign devil"* and Western Imperialism. The young people were especially disillusioned by this event which led to street riots and the founding of the May 4th movement. The eyes of the youth and the intellectuals then turned from the West to the Russian revolution. One of those clever young people at the time was Mao Zedong who was involved in the founding of the Communist Party in 1920. What price betrayal?

The treaty was also hard on Germany, and the humiliating conditions imposed contributed to the later rise of Hitler and Fascism.

It is a sad thought that the seed of betrayal and revenge sown from Versailles – the treaty was signed in the hall of mirrors in the Sun King's palace, led to the twin evils of Communism and Fascism, inspiring the rise of Mao Zedong and Hitler.

Few people have heard of the Taiping rebellion -1850-64, and yet it was a pivotal event in forming the mind set of China. In 1850, Hung Hsui-Ch'ian - a dismal civil servant who failed the Confucian exams four times, joined up with a fundamentalist Presbyterian missionary to investigate the claims of Christianity.

The missionary soon split with him, but this man had a perverted religious zeal, thinking he was the brother of Christ. He wanted to see China as a Christian republic and tried replacing the Emperor with a view to turning all of the nation's property over to the people. He was not afraid to use violence to see this happen. The results of this rebellion - and this is hard to believe, was that it became one of the most destructive conflicts in history with up to 30 million people perishing! I'm perpetually amazed at the world's lack of knowledge of such an awesome conflict which is why it is getting a mention in this small introduction to China!

This event occurred only 150 years ago and it helped me to see the potential danger of fanaticism and mass movements in China. This may be one of the major reasons that the government is so wary of religious movements outside of their control.

Anyway, before I get you too bogged down in a treatise on Chinese history, let's get back to the more recent story of my visit.

The well known phrase of Napoleon concerning China as a sleeping giant :

"Leave that giant alone for when it awakes the world will tremble,"

came back to me with force as I stepped onto Chinese ground, after a long flight. The cities are enormous with high rise buildings shooting up on every street corner. New businesses are rapidly gaining ground and Western multinational companies are putting up their well recognised signs.

China is passionately energetic and hungry for progress and goods of all shapes and sizes. It wants its fair share of the world's pie...now!

The population and potential for growth is phenomenal. Hard toiling, low paid workers teemed the streets, while construction men - perched precariously on bamboo scaffolding, were reaching ever higher heavenwards, offering another skyscraper to the gods of materialism. The lethargic West is already showing signs of strain, while China runs eagerly on into its destiny - a destiny that may influence the world for better, or for worse, a destiny that may lie in the vulnerable, wounded lives of the Chinese Christians. The myriad black bunched heads and tear stained eyes of so many kneeling Jesus believers in this land will surely make a significant impact on the history of the world. China imposes itself as a prayer priority on any strategy for global impact.

Meeting up with brothers and sisters in the underground church must count as another one of the greatest privileges of my life. Like most Christian groups in China, they were suffering persecution and their training school had been discovered. Some of the young students had been beaten, tortured and imprisoned.

It was a humbling experience listening to their testimonies. The group were beginning to come around to thinking of a more city based training, revolving around English teaching and computing. While praying together, the Lord impressed on me a prophetic word inspired from Matthew 23:37,

"How often I have longed to gather your children together, as a hen gathers her chicks under her wings."

God valued the persecution and suffering, but it seemed that he was also longing to create a covering which would allow the church to gather and be nurtured. The Chinese church is strong in martyrdom and evangelism - God wanted to care for it as well, as a mother cares for her young.

We prayed much into the *"wings"* which needed to come into place to cover the missionary army in training. Many were inspired by the options of using business as a means to penetrate society and some were setting up an employment agency.

"The kingdom of God is like an employment agency." Matthew 20:1 – my translation!

The Bejing Olympics opened a window on China, giving some Christian groups a chance to gain greater freedoms via the business models and market influence they had established.

After these prayers, our team went home for more of a relaxing social evening. We decided to watch the old Gladys Aylewood film - *"The Inn of the 6th happiness."*

I thought this a most prophetic film, with a young generation being mothered and led over the mountains into the city. Gladys Aylewood became known as Jenai - the one who loves people. The concept of *Jen* is also the centre of Confucian teaching. It is generally taken to be a compassionate love for humanity, or for the world as a whole. What greater missionary incarnation could there be than *Jen* in a heart ?

A teaching seminar had been arranged. I could never understand why such quality men and women should ever want to learn from a cosseted Westerner like myself.

I was the true learner, clumsily holding chopsticks like the worn out theology I was steeped in. After a long train journey, filled with unknown conversation and endless snacks of fruit and rice, we arrived. We met folk and enjoyed wonderful fellowship and hospitality. Just before going to bed, a Chinese leader knelt down and, gently taking a bowl of warm water and a towel, he proceeded to wash my feet. It was to be the last gesture of the conference for me.

Having settled down to pray and to sleep, we were suddenly roused by a sharp knock on the door.

"We have problems. The police are here. You need to go."

We quickly got dressed, grabbed our stuff, and followed our young Chinese colleagues outside. We could hear shouts and the ominous echoes of dogs barking, as torch lights pierced the darkness.

We slipped clumsily through the night, until we reached the home of a kindly older lady. She was willing to hide us, but we felt the risks were too great for her, and decided to make a run for it over the frosty, foggy fields. Our boots were caked with mud and our clothes whitened with the frosty dew. Silently breathless, we ran on for more than two hours, every shadow representing the possibility of arrest and incarceration. The danger was all the more real for our Chinese colleagues who refused to leave us despite our pleas for them to go home.

We eventually managed to flag down a van and take a very round-a-bout trip to a distant railway station which gave us a long train journey back to the safety of a larger town. Although all this was a bit surreal for us, it was only too real for our Chinese colleagues and was part of their everyday lives. Happily, nothing was found and our brothers did not get into any further trouble.

I later learnt that the police had come to the village that particular night searching for bank robbers who had just happened to rob a bank that very evening! In that uncanny co-incidence, we came close to disaster as we could so easily have been mistaken for the robbers as we ran over the fields. It would also have been hard for our Chinese brothers to explain why Westerners were with them in the house. The experience seemed to confirm the necessity to put into place the *"covering wings"* for future ministry trips. It seemed too costly to risk so much for the teaching of a few Westerners.

It was uplifting to be able to join the worship of Chinese brothers and sisters in later meetings. I was challenged by the strength, ministry and commitment of the young ladies in the churches. There is something very beautiful and bride like in the Asian church. This is not to disregard the need to raise up male disciples, but simply the challenge to acknowledge the beauty where it is.

Since the events of that first trip, the door continued to open into this land and December 2001 saw another invitation to teach the growing numbers of hungry missionary candidates.

Jet lagged and cramped after a long flight, I found myself rushed onto another five hour bus trip to the countryside where eager students were awaiting. The bus filled with thick smoke, as nicotine addicted men sucked greedily on their cigarettes, the droning engine noise interrupted only by a guttural chorus of phlegm filled spitting and coughing.

The cold night concealed our arrival, and for seven days I was hidden away in total cultural immersion with the Chinese students who became my family for a few precious days. I needed to sleep with all my clothes on as it was so cold. I had forgotten my sleeping bag, but the students generously supplied me with a rather damp quilt.

"This belonged to one of the students who has since had to leave," they said.

The next morning, having survived a shivering night, I dared to ask why the other student had left.

"Oh! He had a painful skin disease," they answered.

My damp quilt seemed all the more uninviting, but it had been given with such generous abandon that I needed to snuggle up in it, with feigned satisfaction, each night! Sub zero temperatures, with no heating and limited water supplies, could not chill the warmth of fellowship as I poured out multiplied hours of teaching - translated faithfully into Mandarin and recorded onto innumerable cassettes, along with periods of prayer and counselling. The sheer hunger for God's word, which emanated from the students, was incredible. The morning began at 5am, with two hours of prayer, then an hour of worship together, then noodles, then four hours teaching - a pause for more noodles, before another four hour session, followed by a final dose of noodles, before an evening session and then bed!

Some of the students were young men of fifteen, whose love and perseverance for the Lord were unflinching. Their passionate zeal more than made up for the Spartan conditions and long hours which made up the time. One rusty bucket served as a toilet for over fifty people and night visits were to be practised by only the initiated!

One of the many highlights – apart from enjoying noodles and rice, was having the privilege of leading a Chinese man - the husband of one of our hosts, to the Lord.

On a dirty floor, covered in coal dust, he knelt down as I led him in a prayer of repentance. Tears filled his eyes as he received Christ into his heart. Another vital member added to the sleeping giant that is the Chinese Church. Another simple dream redeemed from that lonely Chinese cemetery in northern France. The Chinese Church is stirring, ready to send her thousands *"Back to Jerusalem,"* along the old silk road - penetrating Gospel resistant nations, to hasten the return of the King.

17 Finding Ruth

Since my first steps of innocence, I've been pursuing my missionary journey for the last thirty years. Seasons change, circumstances bring joy or sadness, but the love of God never changes. Often, on this journey, I have found myself crying out to God for a renewed passion and fresh revelation of his goodness.

Moses was also a man on a journey and, after so many years of walking in the dry desert, his heart must have been longing to set foot in the promise land. Psalm 106:23 shows us Moses at his best, interceding for the people and saving them from destruction. Verses 32 & 33 however, show Moses in a less favourable light, as his spirit becomes bitter and frustrated with the people because of their rebellion. My French version translates it,

"They (the people) made him bitter in spirit."

After years of pioneer Christian work in France and other nations, I can identify with Moses best and worst moments!

Moses faced the challenge of *"Meribah"* and *"Massah"* - quarrelling and testing. The constant squabbles and strife amongst brothers, coupled with the onslaughts of cynicism and unbelief, are enough to put *"rash words"* on even the most saintly of lips!

The pressure was strong enough to push even Moses to unbelief and anger - resulting in him falling short of his dream. I'm always glad to see that he finally got to the Promise Land, as we see him mysteriously present at Jesus' transfiguration.

Better or Bitter?

I'm sure that most ministries eventually come to this kind of testing. We can risk becoming cynical and negative, or we can push through into greater victory and brokenness. The testing brings a real cross and, as the years roll past, Paul's words in 2 Corinthians 4 : 10-12,

"Death is at work in us , but life is at work in you,"

become more our experience than just simple theory.

How do you become better when circumstances around cry out for bitterness?

Many years ago, I found myself asking this question, and God seemed to lead me to the beautiful book of Ruth in the Old Testament to challenge and present me with a personal - and dare I say, prophetic answer.

Let's look at the person of Naomi in the book. She might be an image of all the tired ministries amongst us. She is equally an allegory of the tired Western Church - I've not forgotten Israel either! Tragedy strikes and she finds herself under death, bereaved of sons and husband.

How many sons has the Western Church lost through its cruel, intolerant religious wars, and how many more cut down in the prime of life on the killing fields of Flanders during the First World War ? Countless others drift into spiritual death without a shot being fired, seduced by the deceiving decadence of the seemingly free West. In a nutshell, Naomi has lost all hope of fecundity. She is hopelessly, tragically barren! She has lost her inheritance.

Was this her sad destiny? Her original name means *"tenderness, " " charming, "* and *"pleasant, "* - love, grace and joy. These are holy attributes of Christ's Body, the Church, called to fill a world with light and life, but tragically wounded and old before her time.

It seems, whether we like it or not, that the Church in the West is pretty barren and in decline. Naomi has changed her name!

"Don't call me Naomi " she told them." Call me Mara, because the Almighty has made my life very bitter. I went away full, but the Lord has brought me back empty. Why call me Naomi? The Lord has afflicted me ; the Almighty has brought misfortune upon

me. " Ruth 1: 20-21

"Mara," means bitter. As we think of all that happens around Christmas time and the hope it brings, it's sobering to think of Naomi, journeying back to that sacred place to be, *"bitter in Bethlehem."*

Is there hope for her? Is there hope for my own weary heart? Can the Western Church know a new beginning? The answer for Naomi - and for us all, came in two things.

1.   A fresh revelation of Christ as our redeemer. *"Redeem your dreams !"*

Naomi had a friend in Boaz and, as the old song puts it, we have a friend in Jesus.

"That man is our close relative ; he is one of our kinsman-redeemers." Ruth 2: 20

Jesus is our redeemer - the one who can heal history and hearts. The Hebrew *"goël "* – redeemer, is used to describe the *"avenger of blood,"* and also the *"kinsman redeemer"* of property in the Old Testament law. It sums up the double aspect of redemption - salvation and inheritance. May we know a fresh hunger and passion for His presence, and a renewed quest to seize our inheritance.

There is nothing extraordinary or unique in me sharing with you such an encouragement to know more about Jesus. *"Develop your relationship with Jesus,"* is always the spiritual answer we hear coming from books and pulpits. As every Sunday school pupil knows, Jesus is always the answer to everything! However, there was also a more strategic answer for Naomi, and it is our second requirement for her healing.

2.   She Found Ruth, and Ruth clung to Her.

Ruth, whose roots were in the despised, incestuous race of the Moabites, was the answer for Naomi.

What does Ruth represent to me? At least two things.

Young people and new nations.

We must be investing in, and praying for, the next generation. I'm convinced that, even in the face of Satan's destructive onslaught on the youth of nations, God is wanting to bring a powerful missionary revival amongst a new generation of *"Joshuas"* – the young servant of Moses who did his long apprenticeship in the presence of the Lord, and who emerged to succeed Moses in taking the promise land for the people of God. Just as the Jews may have been shocked by Ruth's culture and background, our religious and missionary structures will need to adapt to the adolescent energy and fun of young people. Without realising it, some of our churches and missions look more like adverts for *" Help the Aged "* and *"SAGA "* holidays! I know I am being extreme - and we must always value the older people in our churches who still have so much to contribute, but so many of us are totally out of touch with the real world of young people, with their dreams, temptations and aspirations.

New missionary nations are also emerging, in which the Holy Spirit has been giving tremendous growth to the Church for many years. Make way for the sacrificial martyrs of China, the fervent prayers of Korea, the hungry soul hunters of Ethiopia and the globally generous Brazilians - to name just a few!

As Naomi made space for Ruth in her life, so we will find our future in creating discipleship environments for such global, indigenous mission movements. We will be learners as much as teachers, receivers as much as givers. Again, structures and personal comfort zones will need to change to stand alongside the colourful, potent, raw energy of God expressing himself in many cultures and skins.

A humble Chinese man recently stood in front of over 500 French pastors, urging them to pray for his *"Back to Jerusalem"* vision and the raising up of 100,000 Chinese missionaries. He'd spent much of his life in prison, but spoke out:

"Whatever the circumstances on your life, God's calling does not change."

A young Chinese girl from Paris, who had come with their choir to sing to us, then said how the church had begun in Paris 5 years ago with just 10 members. They now have 500. I also remembered how a French mayor of an inner city district of Paris had said that the people who were doing the most to curb inner city violence were the Black African churches.

In the light of this, my own prayer - and perhaps your own, is very much to be able to find Ruth.

Perhaps you think I've been hard and extreme on the Western Church, and that your own church is wonderfully alive, winning the lost to Christ, sending out missionaries and influencing society for God. If you are indeed such a Caleb, go and take your mountain, seize the territory, but learn to love Ruth as well.

And there in Bethlehem, where Mary was to hold Jesus to her breast, old Naomi finds new life and nurses a son of promise in David's line.

"She took the child , laid him in her lap and cared for him." Ruth 4: 16

She rediscovered her name and was *"blessed in Bethlehem."*

This reminds us of the Christmas child who always brings new hope with the promise of a better future. May you, like Naomi, be blessed in Bethlehem, may you be *"better"* rather than *"bitter"* and may the opportunity Ruth offers be accepted as the true gift to a waiting Church.

"Praise be to the Lord, who this day has not left you without a kinsman-redeemer. May he become famous throughout Israel! He will renew your life and sustain you in your old age. For your daughter- in-law – Ruth, who loves you and who is better to you than seven sons, has given him birth." Ruth 4: 14

18 Love Triumphant

As we've travelled together through the previous pages, a few may be thinking that the tough realities of missionary life have been minimised in favour of the thrilling adventure of living for Christ. Before I respond to this, I'd like you to think of Jacob from the Old Testament. He was running away from the hatred of his brother and found himself working for Laban. His lot was not an easy one as he routinely cared for boring old sheep! He himself sums up his position:

"This was my situation: The heat consumed me in the daytime and the cold at night, and sleep fled from my eyes. It was like this for the twenty years I was in your household." Genesis 31: 40-41

I've also been serving the Lord for the last three decades and, like Jacob, I know what it is to persevere and suffer. However, like Jacob, I also have the same secret.

Jacob was in love with Rachel.

I too, find motivation in a fresh revelation, not of Rachel's love, but of Christ's love. His love for me, and His love for His Bride – the Church. Jacob was so captivated by the beautiful vision of Rachel that he practically forgot the difficulties of his service:

"So Jacob served seven years to get Rachel, but they seemed like only a few days to him because of his love for her." Genesis 29: 20

I've been so captivated by the beauty and grace of the Lord that I've not had time to consider the hard labour and disappointments along the way.

Forgive me for getting so carried away!

However, Jacob had to learn to love Leah as well!

She was not as attractive as Rachel - her weak eyes are a sign of lack of vision. If Rachel was a beautiful vision, then Leah represented hard-nosed reality. Rachel remained sterile whilst Leah was a fruit bearer. Although it's easy to fall in love with vision, we must also embrace our realities - for it is they that lead us to fruitfulness. The vision without reality leads to sterility. However, Jacob learnt to love Leah and eventually saw the fruitfulness of Rachel. If we persevere in the service and humility of reality, our vision will eventually bear fruit.

I too, have learnt to love Leah over the years. Africa and France are good places to meet her. Years of working in teams and leading churches has also shown me Leah in all her shapes and sizes.

A bloody cross always precedes a resurrection. Death, division and tragedy are all around us in this sad, sin stained, world.

One tragic day in Africa, a young lady came to see me to pour out her heart. To be able to survive and bring up her baby girl, she had to sell her body as a prostitute. This sordid trade sowed the seed of a new baby into her and she found herself pregnant. The baby grew inside of her along with the panic and worry of another mouth to feed. Tired and alone, she reached the time of birth. She screamed in her dark and bloody loneliness and gave birth to another tiny, African child. The darkness of poverty and shame put madness into her already fragile mind and her fingers tightened around the screaming child's neck. She squeezed and squeezed and then there was silence. A mother murdered her new born babe. No one saw, no one knew and no one seemed to care. She gathered the small limp body, cleaned up the blood and mess, dug an anonymous hole in the ground and threw the dead baby in - from womb to tomb in a few short tragic moments. Earth covered the deed, but the deep scars of guilt were not so easily covered over.

Whose guilt ? Sin always flows down from the top to land on the weakest and most innocent. It would be hard to measure the deep suffering and tears that flowed from both European and African eyes as a measure of healing, justice and redemption was clumsily applied to so deep a tragedy.

I could go on. Our first attempts to build a self-help business in Africa met with the sudden death, through the tragedy of A.I.D.S, of the founding member. Coups, road accidents, ethnic violence and disease have only too often demanded a high price from suffering hearts. I can never forget the tears of African intercessors.

The indifference and apathetic decadence of the Christian, civilised West is less visibly shocking, but no less destructive. I've known what it is to be rejected for one's faith. The secular mind set of France easily brands enthusiasm for Christ as a cultic deviation. The pain of division - when close friends are separated by demonically inspired traps, is a deep wound to bear. Joseph's dreams were rejected by his jealous brothers, and so often *"the brothers"* in the Church family reject those with the multi coloured missionary cloaks.

Every day life can also be cruel. Children are born less than perfect, Alzheimer's disease brings a slow and undignified end to the most noble of brains. Adolescent children can rebel, bringing worry and doubt to a family. Personal weaknesses and fears bring discouragement, while habitual sin clings and follows like some unwanted, mangy dog. The list goes on.

So, having embraced Leah, what do you do?

I play with a ping pong ball in the bath! Let me explain.

Like some modern day Archimedes, I like to splash around and philosophise. I like to take hold of the ball and draw it down to the depths of the bath. Submerged and hidden under the weight of water, there is still a dynamic energy, longing to pull the ball back to the surface. In fact, the deeper you take the ball down, the stronger the upwards pull becomes. Think of Christ for a moment. The Apostle Paul tells us that Christ,

"Descended to the lower earthly regions."

Like some living, divine, cosmic *"ping pong ball,"* he descended from the heights of heaven to take the lowest, most shameful place of suffering. He went under to the very depths of hell. Like a modern day Jonah, he was *"hurled into the deep,"* tasting the profound suffering of humanity in all its madness, lostness and despair. The waves and breakers of a world's accumulated sin bore down on his vulnerable innocence, bringing total

154

brokenness.

The world's philosophers - from Plato and the Greeks, to the existentialist *"nausea"* of Sartre. The world's religions and regimes - where Pharaohs, Priests and Prophets, like Mao, Marx or Confucius speak their wisdom. The New Age Gurus of reincarnation and revamped Hinduism. All sink like lead, to remain in heavy hopelessness, in the depths of human sin and suffering.

Only one man was truly *"upwardly mobile."*

"He who descended is the very one who ascended higher than all the heavens, in order to fill the whole universe." Ephesians 4: 9

Christ was full of the breath of God, the air of heaven - the power of love. Life and generosity so filled him, that he naturally broke forth into the reality of resurrection and overcoming life.

"That power is like the working of his mighty strength , which he exerted in Christ when he raised him from the dead and seated him at his right hand in the heavenly realms, far above all rule and authority, power and dominion, and every title that can be given, not only in the present age but also in the one to come." Ephesians 1: 19-21

Christ is indeed our only hope, and the only one who triumphs over death and sin. Knowledge of his love and power enables us to embrace the harsh realities of this world, where innocence dies daily.

My prayer for all who have arrived at this last chapter, is that you may deeply know Christ - that this relation may enable the breath of the Holy Spirit to fill your own little *"ping pong ball"* hearts, making you too, *"upwardly mobile,"* as you face the pressures of sin and death.

"I pray also that the eyes of your heart may be enlightened in order that you may know the hope to which he called you, the riches of his glorious inheritance in the saints, and his incomparably great power for us who believe." Ephesians 1: 18-19

The famous German writer, Thomas Mann, at the end of his long novel, *"The Magic Mountain,"* which seeks to understand modern man's situation in the world, ended with these lines:

"Moments there were, when out of death and the rebellion of the flesh, there came to thee, as thou tookest stock of thyself, a dream of love. Out of this universal feast of death, out of this extremity of fever, kindling the rain-washed evening sky to a fiery glow may it be that love one day shall mount?"

May such love mount in the face of the risen Christ.

So, at the end of the book, I may have found the original answer that my Dad shared with me all those years ago. I remember how a reflexion of that ultimate love also mounted in his eyes as he shared the meaning to life that he had discovered.

"Lots of loving!"

A Final Word

This is a book that has been a long time in coming to press. Fourteen years have passed since its inception. As I've come back to it, and read its contents, I've been overwhelmed by the innocent power and conviction of first love.

I have been tempted to re-write the whole thing, adding more stories and testimonies of all that the Lord continues to do amongst the nations. Many of the tiny seeds, sown in the early years of this book, have since grown to become mighty trees, giving a home to many *"birds of the air"* who have found a refuge. New works have begun and been established in Ethiopia, Rwanda, Indonesia, and beyond. New stories await their time to be told. The world has become a different place, and I too have changed. Like some long planted tree, I have more rings of age defining my existence.

I am encouraged by the first *"steps of innocence"* this book reminds me of. It calls me back to my first love and untrammelled faith. It is a book I could no longer write – not because there is anything untrue or unsound, but because my own capacity to innocence has been tempered with the fires of life and wisdom. *"Steps of Experience,"* might well be a fitting sequel, as the young man of innocence has grown a few grey hairs.

It carries the pioneer spirit of a slower, less complicated season of life. It also carries the prophetic call to *"Love Ruth."* May our years be given to this quest of encouraging the new emerging missionary movements that are arising around the world. May we empower and encourage the host of young people waiting to discover their dreams.

About the Author

I am a child, animal, poet and saint – with a very small 's'.

The child laughs. He enjoys life in all its simplicity and innocence, longing to share the joy with those he loves. The animal embraces the gift of natural instinct, running to survive, blissfully at home in the gift of creation. The poet savours intimate words of the divine and delights in writing. The saint thrives on the intimacy of Christ which thrusts him out to find meaning and purpose in the world. He encourages through preaching the whispers of heaven he has faintly overheard.

www.he-sed.com

Made in the USA
Charleston, SC
21 November 2015